# Praise for Bill Clegg's
## *Ninety Days*

### *Named one of the Best Books of 2012 by the* Huffington Post

"A raw, honest, and very well-written tale of alcoholism and drug abuse." —Andrew Losowsky, *Huffington Post*

"Addiction is a lethal business, and we often forget, reading a survivor's account, the frequent mortal cost of drug use. Bill Clegg doesn't forget that the addict's will to live must be committed to each day. His memoir of crack use and recovery is written to fellow users dead or no longer around, the disappeared and soon-to-be-gone, as well as to those who have re-emerged with him.... Clegg's need to connect saves him.... What he has now—fewer secrets, gratitude, relief, an acknowledgment of his vulnerability, time out from his dance with death—adds up, like days."
—Michael Stein, *San Francisco Chronicle*

"Honest and earnest." —Mike Vilensky, *Wall Street Journal*

"Relationships, rather than high drama, are the real focus of *Ninety Days,* and as a result there is a tenderness at its heart.... Clegg reveals it is people... that keep him afloat."

—Molly Creeden, Vogue.com

"Bill Clegg drops the reader inside the mind of a man desperately hoping to stay clean, navigating a city that once was so hospitable to his urges, and finding a community of road-sharers who he learns to trust and shoulder. A lot can go wrong with a recovery memoir, but Clegg has a direct, spare style and an engaging voice that is reminiscent, at least to me, of Jean Rhys in her fictional addiction book *Good Morning, Midnight.* It is because of this immediacy that *Ninety Days* turns out to be such an exhilarating story of *ascent.*"

—Christopher Bollen, *Interview Magazine*

"With his dazzling new memoir, *Ninety Days,* the literary wunderkind discovers that hitting rock bottom can be the easiest part of addiction. The tricky part is staying in recovery.... An intimate view of what happens after rehab, as the young addict returns to his old stomping grounds and struggles to let go of everything he lost... and press reset."

—Mike Guy, *The Fix*

"Clegg has done something singular and unique in the literature of recovery. He has made *relapse* the subject and not *re-*

*covery* the subject. That self-proclaimed emphasis is this book's great strength because the question posed from the very beginning of whether or not he's going to do crack again or drink again is never really answered. In a large way, this is a book about *not* finding the answer, when most memoirs are poised to do the exact opposite....Sobriety isn't promised, nor is it unattainable, and Bill Clegg knows better than any writer I've ever read on the subject the delicate difference between the two."　　　　　　　　—Michael Klein, *Lambda Literary*

"Clegg follows his gut-wrenching *Portrait of an Addict as a Young Man* with an equally stark tale of the hard and ongoing work of recovering from addiction."

—Vanessa Bush, *Booklist*

"The author writes with astonishing honesty, infusing the intensely interior narrative with powerful imagery and penetrating insights. Even the short journeys to his daily support groups sound like heroic odysseys....The outcome is never assured, and there are casualties among the sharply drawn characters, most of whom the author seems to know as intimately as his own psyche. Three scant months may not seem like a long time, but for all involved it was an epic period of transformation. At turns cautionary and inspirational, Clegg's saga embraces both the weaknesses and strengths of human nature, while only alluding to the possibility of salvation. A gritty, lyrical, and potent portrait of what it really means to be addicted." —*Kirkus Reviews*

"Clegg has rebuilt his career as an agent and become one of the best-known faces of addiction recovery.... *Ninety Days*, written in straightforward, readable prose, is an often-vivid testament to the difficulties of overcoming addiction and the value of companionship.... Clegg comes across as a deeply troubled but perceptive and sympathetic man, learning lessons about addiction in some very difficult ways." —Thomas Rogers, *Salon*

"A prescient, superbly crafted glimpse of the frighteningly long-shot odds.... Sharp, taut block paragraphs in a stripped-down present tense that creates an unflinching immediacy.... Clegg re-ups and delivers one last sucker punch in the book's final pages, one last reminder that recovery never really ends. If anything, this bleak meditation on human frailty serves as a much-needed reminder that as easy as it is to stumble, there will always be a pair of hands that have been bruised just as badly waiting to pull us back up." —Christopher Vola, *PopMatters*

"Clegg's spare, nearly minimalist style complements the drama inherent in his material: it's addition through subtraction.... With understated craft, Clegg has written a harrowing story." —*Publishers Weekly*

"When Bill Clegg's first memoir, *Portrait of an Addict as a Young Man*, came out in 2010, it resonated because it was the story of a relatable, successful man... who lost it all to crack addiction. And, then, somehow, managed to write a book that seemed less manipulative, far more earnest, than many addiction memoirs on bookshelves today.... As a follow-up to his first book, *Ninety Days* describes recovery and eventual relapse, stopping short of 2012, when he seems to have put the pieces pretty squarely back together."

—Kurt Soller, *Esquire*

"This is a memoir about how difficult it is to achieve and maintain sobriety, and Clegg's ultimate realization that it cannot be accomplished on one's own. Standing out among the many similar works on addiction and recovery, Clegg's intellectual story of his never-ending struggle for sobriety and his heartfelt, passionate revelations will directly touch the hearts of readers. "

—*Library Journal*

"Whatever you know about addictions, *Ninety Days* will broaden your knowledge and understanding. There are no excuses or minimizing of the problems; Clegg opens himself up as is necessary for long-term recovery."

—Maggie Harding, Bookreporter.com

"Perhaps most affecting is the advice he takes from his sponsor in a moment of desperation: 'Pray,' the man urges him, 'because whatever you've been doing isn't working.' "

—Mallory Rice, *Nylon*

"In *Portrait of an Addict as a Young Man*, Clegg detailed his descent from high-powered literary agent to full-time alcoholic and crackhead. This sequel is about his recovery—the circular pattern of stupefyingly tedious rehab and harrowing relapse. And yet it's suspenseful: We come to care about Clegg, whose voice is engaging and who never gets mired in self-pity."

—Mike Doherty, *National Post*

"More than the saga of his recovery, *Ninety Days* is the story of his embrace of the methodology of recovery: its mores, credos, precepts. In the final pages of *Portrait*, he had noted a stirring of his feelings toward 'something less self-concerned.' He has delivered on this stirring by writing a memoir that is an ode to a community. It is 'the flip side' of his crack paranoia. He does not 'count days' alone."

—James Camp, *New York Observer*

"Despite the squalor and the stupors and the black maelstroms of self-doubt, Clegg's prose is mercifully limpid. His whole account is clear-eyed, rarely foggy on recollection and never once unstinting in presentation. This warts-and-all approach renders his memoir plausible and helps transform it into a cautionary tale, though one that doesn't lecture, just bluntly states its sad case. *Ninety Days* is memoir as journey, and we find ourselves rooting for Clegg all the way—every last lucky, lonely, destructive, delusional, selfish, wretched, insane, desperate second of it.... We appreciate it all the more for being a bumpy ride: it is sobering, yes, but also superb, and...utterly redemptive."                                        —Malcolm Forbes, *The Rumpus*

# NINETY DAYS

ALSO BY BILL CLEGG

*Portrait of an Addict as a Young Man*

# NINETY
# DAYS

*A Memoir of Recovery*

# BILL CLEGG

BACK BAY BOOKS
Little, Brown and Company
*New York  Boston  London*

Copyright © 2012 by Bill Clegg
Reading group guide copyright © 2013 by Bill Clegg and Little, Brown and Company

Back Bay Books / Little, Brown and Company
Hachette Book Group
1290 Avenue of the Americas, New York, NY 10104
littlebrown.com

Originally published in hardcover by Little, Brown and Company, April 2012
First Back Bay paperback edition, April 2013

Back Bay Books is an imprint of Little, Brown and Company, a division of Hachette Book Group, Inc. The Back Bay Books name and logo are trademarks of Hachette Book Group, Inc.

The publisher is not responsible for websites (or their content) that are not owned by the publisher.

The Hachette Speakers Bureau provides a wide range of authors for speaking events. To find out more, go to hachettespeakersbureau.com or call (866) 376-6591.

Excerpt from *Seasonal Rights* by Daniel Halpern, copyright © 1979, 1980, 1981, 1982 by Daniel Halpern. Used by permission of Viking Penguin, a division of Penguin Group (USA) Inc.

Library of Congress Cataloging-in-Publication Data
Clegg, Bill.
Ninety days : a memoir of recovery / Bill Clegg.—1st ed.
    p. cm.
ISBN 978-0-316-12252-8 (hc) / 978-0-316-12254-2 (pb)
1. Clegg, Bill. 2. Drug addicts—United States—Biography. 3. Literary agents—United States—Biography. I. Title.
HV5805.C595A3 2011
362.29092—dc23
[B]                                                        2011032542

*For Polly, Annie, Jack & Asa*
*and Everyone Counting Days*

As snow fills the places
where you must have walked,
you start back to where you began,
that place you again prepare to leave,
alone and warm, again intact, starting out.

     —Daniel Halpern, from "White Field"


Forget yourself.

        —Henry Miller

# Contents

# Contents

# NINETY DAYS

# Borrow Mine

It looks like Oz. This is what I think as Manhattan comes into view through the windshield of Dave's jeep. The crowded towers poke the sky with their metal and glass and in the midday haze look faraway, mythic, more idea than place. We're driving in thick traffic that moves swiftly and in unison. A month ago I hadn't noticed the city receding behind us as we drove from Lenox Hill Hospital to the rehab in White Plains. We didn't talk much then and we're not talking much now.

Dave is playing music I don't recognize. A charcoal-voiced girl is crying with as much earnestness as irony alongside an acoustic guitar. He tells me her name and it sounds more like a department store than a person. He compares her to another singer I don't know, and I feel as if I've lost fluency in a language that once was second nature. Between Lenox Hill and rehab I've been in treatment for six weeks, but it seems like years, and I imagine during that time new bands coming and going, movies capturing the attention of the masses and being forgotten, books sparking controversy or indifference, and the roar of it all fading to make way for new entries in the cultural lottery. Dave tells me about a play he and Susie have just seen and I feel myself shrinking in the seat, becoming kid-sized. Up ahead, Oz juts higher above the horizon.

It's early April, a Monday. We're driving to Dave's writing studio on Charles Street in the West Village. He's offered me the place for a few weeks while I find somewhere to live. I've just finished four weeks in a small drug and alcohol rehab on the grounds of an old mental asylum. Dave drove me there after I was released from the psych ward at Lenox Hill Hospital, where I wound up after a two-month bender that ended in a fistful of sleeping pills, a bottle of vodka, a crack pipe stuffed to bursting, and an ambulance. The small literary agency I co-owned and ran for four years is gone, all my clients have found new agents, our employees have scattered to new jobs or left New York, and whatever money I once had has been wiped out, leaving in its place a rising debt of legal, hospital, and rehab bills. The eight-year relationship with my boyfriend, Noah, is over, and the apartment at One Fifth Avenue his grandmother bought him, where we lived for six years, is no longer my home. I can sleep at Dave's office, but I have to be out between ten and five so he can work.

The song changes—the girl is talking more than singing, the guitar is now a cello—and I wonder what I'll do all day, how I'll fill up the hours, where I'll go.

*Sure you want to do this?* Dave asks cautiously. *Sure you should be coming back here?* He turns the music down and keeps his eyes on the road while he voices my own doubts. I'm not sure of anything. I'm thirty-four years old. Unemployed. Unemployable in a field I worked in for twelve years. I have a mountain of terrifying paper waiting for me: the settlement agreement with my ex–business partner, Kate, dismantling the agency; bills from my lawyers; hospital bills and insurance forms; e-mails and letters—angry, loving, and everything in between—from friends, former colleagues, and family. The balance of the rehab bill is at least forty thousand dollars and likely much more. My sister Kim, who lives in Maine, in the midst of picking up and dropping off her twin boys from school, play dates, and baseball practice, has taken over the bills, the accounts, the lawyer, and our plan is to go over every last difficult bit of it once I'm settled in at Dave's.

I've arranged to see my sponsor, Jack, at an evening meeting in the West Village—*a beginner's meeting* is how he describes it. I first met Jack on the third or fourth day in the hospital. After a rough, shame-shocked start there when I refused to see or speak to anyone, I eventually agreed to meet him—a friend of a friend, my age, curly haired, boyish, gay—and he offered to be my sponsor, a sort of coach/big brother/guide, in a fellowship for people with alcoholism and drug addiction. I learned later, in rehab, that there are many fellowships—some free, some not, most with organized meetings—where people go for help with addictions like mine. The one Jack belongs to is the one I join.

Dave pulls up in front of an old ivy-covered apartment building on Charles Street between Bleecker and West 4th. I step onto the sidewalk and wait while he makes a phone call from the front seat. It's quiet. The air is humid and the streets are speckled with afternoon light. A young, high-cheekboned couple walk by, speaking what sounds like Russian into their cell phones. A fire engine wails. A trim young man with a Great Dane on a leash bends with a plastic bag in hand to scoop up a pile of the elegant dog's poop. *New York*, I think. *I'm back in New York*. I see a middle-aged man walking alone with an earpiece connected to a wire that disappears into his tan windbreaker. He looks at me a beat too long and a little too seriously and an old familiar panic flashes in my chest. Dave comes around to the side of the jeep and grabs two bags from the back and barks, *C'mon, I have to meet Susie*. I rush to help, and when I turn to look for the tan-jacketed man, he's gone.

I follow Dave up three flights of exceedingly creaky stairs as he tells me how the old woman on the second floor, just below his studio, is highly sensitive, extremely cranky, and will call him day or night if she feels anything is awry. I wonder if this is his way of discouraging any funny business. A little barricade against what he and everyone else in my life fear will happen now that I've returned to New York: relapse.

The apartment is a bright studio with a fireplace, high ceilings, and a small, dangling crystal chandelier. It looks like the study in a much larger, very nice old house. Dave's books line the mantel and shelves, and there are old rugs scattered about. The small brown couch unfolds into a bed

that I'll sleep on for the next few weeks. Dave rat-a-tat-
tats a tour of the basics—towels, locks, a pile of blankets,
tricky windows, cutlery, cups, coffee machine, keys—and
then he's gone. I had imagined having coffee with him at a
nearby café and a brotherly speech about how it's all going to
work out—that I have to be brave, that I can count on him,
et cetera—but what he offers instead is help with the bags,
another warning about the downstairs neighbor, a worried
look, and a hurried good-bye.

The apartment looks onto a garden behind a town house. It's
a minimalist oasis: boxwood, teak, reflecting pool. The town
house has large clear panes of glass that frame exquisite mid-
century modern furniture on the second floor, and a clean
geometry of stainless steel, marble, and what looks like suede
in the kitchen below. Order and wealth hum from the place
and I can barely look. I close my eyes and only then do I
hear the bright racket of songbirds. They sound exactly like
the birds that covered the trees near the field where I walked
on the grounds in rehab. I imagine a flock flying just above
Dave's jeep the whole way down from White Plains, de-
scending now upon the branches outside to chirp and coo
their encouragement.

*Hi guys,* I say and am startled by the sound of my voice. *Thanks for the welcome home party,* I whisper, and though I'm embarrassed by the fantasy of the birds escorting me back to New York, I'm still glad for any kindness—made up, even—coming from the greenery outside. I lie down on the couch and listen.

The birds carry on. Voices drift in from outside. The refrigerator hums in the little kitchen. And all at once it hits me: I'm alone. No one besides Dave knows exactly where I am. I could be doing anything. I've been in-patient for weeks, under the thumb of nurses and doctors and counselors the entire time. No more morning gatherings, group meals, and in-bed-by-ten room checks. I'm alone and unaccountable. And then, like a dead ember blown to life, I think about my old dealers, Rico and Happy. I remember how I owe each of them a thousand dollars and wonder—despite all that's been lost, everyone hurt, despite everything—how I'm going to get two grand to pay these guys off so I can buy more. I start to puzzle through credit cards and PIN codes for cash advances. Suddenly a few thousand dollars seems within reach and I can feel that old burn, that hibernating want, come awake. I imagine the relief that first hit will deliver and I'm suddenly up off the couch and pacing. *No no no,* I chant. *No fucking way.* That craving, once it begins, is almost impossible to reverse. What my addict mind imagines, my addict body chases. It's like Bruce Banner as he's turning into the Incredible Hulk. Once his muscles begin to strain against his clothes and his skin goes green, he has no choice but to let the monster spring from him and unleash its inevitable damage.

I step on a creaky floorboard and remember the old lady below. I think of Dave and how he's spent most of his day driving to White Plains and back; how he's trusting me with his place, and how worried he looked when he left. I look at my watch. It's 3:50 and I remember Jack had suggested I go to a four o'clock meeting around the corner if I returned to the city in time. *I can make it,* I think desperately, meaning both the meeting and in general. I grab the set of keys from the mantel and, as gently as I can, descend the three flights of noisy stairs and hurry out to the street.

By the time I get to the meeting it's packed and I have to wedge myself through the crowd to grab what looks like the last seat. I sit down against a wall painted robin's egg blue and as I do, I see Jack. He's sitting in the seat directly across from mine with a big glad-you-could-make-it smile. We're not supposed to meet until later, but he's surprised me by showing up at my first meeting back in the city. *Welcome home*, he whispers seriously as the lights go down and the meeting begins.

I have met Jack only three times—twice at Lenox Hill and once during the last week at rehab when we went for a long walk and sat in a white gazebo and listened to the head counselor say he believed I was someone who would make it, someone he didn't see relapsing. Jack is a music critic and lives in the city with his boyfriend. He wasn't a crack addict, but his history with drugs and alcohol reminds me of my own, and every time I think I've told him something too embarrassing or too shameful, he's quick with a story that reminds me we've sunk to the same depths. I keep needing to remind myself that Jack is a drug addict. He's so put together, so clear-eyed and wholesome. It surprises me when he describes doing things when he was high that I'm convinced no one else but me has done. Like hitting on taxicab drivers. He tells me this the first time we meet at Lenox Hill, when I'm still paranoid about being followed by undercover DEA agents. My first response is *How did you know?* To which he responds, *What do you mean? I was there!* And after a beat I understand that he was there when *he* had done it, not when I had.

The meeting ends and we go for coffee. I tell him about the craving I had an hour ago in Dave's apartment. He tells me if it happens again—*and it will*—I need to immediately call him or someone else who is sober. If I get his voice mail I should leave messages describing what's going on, even if it's to say I plan on getting drugs or that I'm about to drink. Just speak it through and then once I've done that, if I can, try to imagine every beat of what will follow. Paying the dealer. Scoring the drugs. Getting high until the drugs are gone and then calling the dealer for more. And more. Running out of money. Getting paranoid. Not picking up the phone when worried friends call. The next day. The horror of morning. The empty bank account. The need to get more. Do more. And on and on.

Back at Dave's a few hours ago, I hadn't imagined anything beyond getting high. Just the high. As we now sit in a crowded coffee shop on Jane Street and talk through where it would lead, I can feel the once-hot little ember of craving cool down. As we talk I wish I could go home with Jack. Move in with him and his boyfriend, at least until I have ninety days clean, which is just a month away. Ninety days is a milestone that many fellowships and organizations dealing with alcohol and substance abuse use to mark a strong foothold in sobriety. Many suggest what I've heard Jack refer to a few times as a *ninety-in-ninety,* which means going to ninety meetings in ninety days. Jack has recommended, since I'm not working and have little else to do, that I go to two meetings a day. At least. The meetings are excruciating sometimes. I have a hard time keeping focused, keeping my mind off how I'm going to figure out and fix my living situation, my finances, and nearly every relationship I have. I can't imagine how I'll make it through two meetings a day for ninety days. *One meeting at a time, one day at a time,* Jack chants when I tell him my worry and it shuts me up. Reaching ninety days has become an important focus of our talks, and though I can't imagine sitting through all those meetings, listening to all those drunks and addicts, can't imagine a future or how I'll sort out the huge mess that is my life, I can sometimes see ahead to ninety days. Jack has even suggested that until I have ninety days I should resist reconnecting with too many people in the city, avoid engaging too much in sorting through the business and financial wreckage. The simplicity of reaching ninety days is calming, and when my head swarms with everything that's happened and everything that might, I think, *Ninety days, ninety days.* Eventually it's all I can see, the only thing before me that needs to be done.

When I'm speaking with Jack I often don't feel the now-usual panic about not having money, a job, or any idea about what I will do with my life. He metabolizes what I imagine are insurmountable obstacles into simple phrases like *One day at a time* and *Take it easy*, which I find at once baffling, patronizing, and comforting. He tells me to have faith that everything has happened just as it's supposed to and that if I just stay sober it will all turn out OK, that before I know it I'll be helping someone else get and stay sober. Help someone else? *Not likely,* I tell him. How can I? I have absolutely nothing to offer. And faith? I don't have any. Certainly not in myself or in any grand design that makes what has happened and what I've done over the last few months and the years leading up to them acceptable. When I tell him I don't have much faith, he says simply, *Borrow mine.*

After coffee, Jack takes me to another meeting of the same organization, a few blocks away, in the basement of a beautiful old brick church. It's the meeting, he says, where he got sober. The one he goes to still. As we head back through the courtyard toward the meeting, we bump into a few people who nod hello to Jack, sometimes giving him a gentle hug and moving on. He smiles and waves to several others and as he leads me toward the front row I feel proud to be with him. It strikes me then, as it has before, that I barely know him. I don't know his boyfriend's name, most of his friends, or where he lives in the city, but I imagine him a sober superhero, a kind of Clark Kent by day and Super Sponsor by night. I look around the room at the dozens and dozens of people sitting in folding chairs—sipping coffee, talking, waiting for the meeting to begin—and no one seems as attractive and confident and kind as Jack does. I'm overwhelmed with gratitude that he stepped into my life when he did. We've spoken on the phone at least once a day since Lenox Hill, and he's talked me through a whole universe of panics. *What a miracle this guy is,* I think, and as I do he tells me I need to raise my hand during the meeting and let the whole room know that I just got out of rehab and that this is my first day back in town.

There are over fifty people in the room. There were only four other patients in rehab, so the group meetings were never this large or remotely this intimidating. I shake my head no and Jack leans in and says, *You don't have a choice. We had a deal: As long as you follow my suggestions, I'm your sponsor. If you don't, I'm not.* And so, a few minutes later, when the guy running the meeting asks if there is anyone in the room under ninety days, I raise my hand and do what I'm told.

The meeting ends and many people, mostly men and gay at that, linger in the courtyard afterwards. Within a minute, a group of guys—young, skinny, with exquisite hair and many, I notice, wearing white belts—come over to say hi. They welcome me and ask if I would like to join them for dinner. *Thanks,* I say graciously, *but I'm having dinner with my sponsor.* But when the last word is out of my mouth I hear Jack behind me saying, *No you're not.* I turn to look at him and see the stern face of a parent ditching his kid at sleep-away camp. Before I can say another word he gives me a hug and tells me to leave him a message on his voice mail when I get home. As I watch him go I consider sneaking back to Charles Street, but too many people are introducing themselves, handing me their phone numbers scrawled on little scraps of paper, for me to be able to disappear unnoticed.

So I go to dinner. The group consists of fifteen guys at least. All gay. Most young. Some cute. Most not. All loud. As we walk toward Chelsea I try to lag behind so it doesn't appear that I'm with them, but each time I do someone drops back to chat with me. *How much time do you have?* is the usual question and I answer, *Fifty-nine days.* I'm embarrassed to tell them my story so I just allude to a rough patch. They seem to get it and don't press.

Eventually we end up at the New Venus diner in Chelsea, where the waiters shove a bunch of tables together to form one long one at the front of the restaurant. In the scuffle of who-sits-where, I wind up toward the end, near the door. As I take my seat, I see a tall, pale guy with red hair and a white Izod shirt sit down directly across from me. He looks Scottish, but too exotic to be Scottish. Maybe Scandinavian, I think, but then wonder if there are red-haired Scandinavians. He's very fit, very pale, loaded with freckles, and his clothes seem to glow they are so clean. *Hi*, he says. *I'm Asa.*

Asa is a few years younger than I am, in graduate school for urban planning, and has been sober three years from a heroin addiction that wiped out his savings and forced him to drop out of school. When I ask him about the red hair he tells me it's a mystery, no one in his family has it, just as no one in his family is an alcoholic or addict. He was raised in what he describes as an eccentric Presbyterian household in Baltimore, but unless there is a meeting being held in one, he no longer goes to church. He seems too well educated and serious for this gaggle of former club kids, but he couldn't appear more comfortable in their company. I tell him my story and he listens and nods and asks the occasional question. I worry that he thinks I'm making up the parts about the agency, Noah, the life I once had, and the two months in hotel rooms that ended it. But at the same time I don't want him to think that I'm trying to impress or shock him. I want to tell him I wasn't always this pathetic, this broken, that it took a long time to get here and no one saw it happening. No one, that is, except Noah. When I hear myself say I used to go to London a lot, I realize I *am* trying to impress him and shut up.

Dinner ends and we talk on the corner of 22nd Street and Eighth Avenue as one by one the sweet, noisy boys I'm embarrassed to be seen with disappear into the night. *Call me,* most say, but I've already thrown out their numbers in the bathroom at the diner. Asa, I've decided, is the one I can relate to. He has the same cautious, easy-does-it tone that Jack has but he's less distant, softer. He tells me about a meeting I should try. Everyone calls it The Library because it's located in some kind of research library and, it turns out, it's a few blocks from One Fifth, where I lived with Noah until two months ago. He describes the people there as a mix of gay and straight, educated and not, all very serious about sobriety. He gives me the address—which I write down on the slip of paper where I've written Dave's Charles Street address—and tells me to meet him there tomorrow, ten minutes before the 12:30 meeting.

It's late. Midnight or after. We walk a few blocks and I say good-bye to Asa on the corner of 17th Street and Eighth Avenue. *I'll see you at the meeting*, he says and reminds me again where it is and when. *Absolutely*, I say, pathetically grateful I have somewhere to go tomorrow, someone to meet. I realize that beyond this and dinner with my friend Jean later in the week, I have no plans. No lunches, dinner parties, movie dates, plays, concerts, conference calls, business trips, breakfast meetings. Nothing. Asa gives me a hug and walks east down 17th Street. I watch him go, watch his white shirt and red hair bob through the dark until they disappear.

I get lost on my way back to Dave's writing studio on Charles Street. I'm not familiar with the West Village even though I've lived four blocks east of here for six years and a few blocks north for three. The streets jumble together, and after going this way and that, each time I'm convinced I've finally figured out where I am, I stumble—again and then again—onto Seventh Avenue. It's as if a spell has been cast and I'm doomed to end up there no matter what route I take. I'm exhausted and consider hailing a cab but I'm too broke and too embarrassed to ask for a ride that may be only one block. I feel as if I'm twenty-one again and have just moved to New York from Connecticut. I'm lost, have no apartment, no job, no family, no spouse. No one is expecting me. Every

lit window taunts with the smug glow of an enviable life.
Through heavy drapes and tasseled blinds I see the edges
of beautiful living rooms shining with lamps and polished
wood, perfectly littered with framed but not yet hung art and
piles of books. Couples scurry home, leaning into each other,
whispering stories and stressing opinions. *Do they know how
lucky they are?* I think as they rush toward what I imagine
are paid-for, mortgage-less, rent-free apartments and town
houses. I watch them and wonder what Noah is doing. My
chest tightens as I picture him winding down the evening
with someone else, the two of them returning home together
as we had countless times. I imagine him telling the story of
his awful addict ex-boyfriend for the first time to astonished,
sympathetic ears.

I finally end up back on Charles Street. All the buildings look
the same, so I double-check the scrap of paper to make sure I
have the right address. It's now almost one o'clock and every
light in the building is off. I fiddle with the lock, turn the key,
and, as softly as I can, enter the vestibule. I take my shoes
off—gently, quietly—and toe the first step. The wood beneath the carpet croaks like the loudest frog. How can I
ascend these stairs without making a racket? How do I get
back to the safe, chandeliered little apartment without waking the whole building? I climb the second and third steps

and they're even louder than the first. I'm sure the woman on the second floor is already calling Dave. Telling him that the hooligan staying in his apartment is thrashing in the stairwell, waking everyone. I can almost hear Dave cursing to Susie, swearing to her that this is the last straw, that he can no longer help me and I will need to find somewhere else to crash while I get back on my feet.

I go slowly. I stop and start dozens of times on the stairs and rest even longer on the first- and second-floor landings. I'm almost to the third floor, nearly at the top of the last flight, when I lose my grip on one of the shoes and—*oh God no*—it falls and bangs loudly down the entire flight of stairs. When it finally smacks against the landing below I freeze and listen for footfalls, creaking floorboards, any signs of suddenly awake tenants. A few minutes pass and with my breath held I reach up and place the remaining shoe at the top of the stairs so I don't drop it. I inch back down until I reach the landing. The steps creak and belch the whole way and my progress—with numerous stops and starts—is excruciatingly slow. I pick up the renegade shoe and squeeze and twist and shake the thing viciously to punish it for causing so much trouble.

I turn back and look up the narrow flight of stairs to the third-floor landing. Nothing has ever seemed so far away. I consider going to sleep right where I stand. I can't bear the sound of another plank of wood screaming under my feet. How did I end up here? Homeless, broke, alone, and frozen with panic on the second-floor landing of someone else's building? How will I ever put my life back together? I stand very still.

Shaking off the drowsiness that's tugging my eyes closed and making my body sag against the wall, I try to be hopeful. The apartment is only one more flight. If I'm quiet enough no one will hear me. If I'm careful enough no one will be angry. The air is damp in the stairwell and my shirt is soaked through with sweat. I imagine everyone in the city safely tucked away in their beds. I wonder again if Noah is alone or with someone. I think of the thirty-one days I have to go until I reach ninety and decide, ominously, that it's easier to count days in psych wards and rehab, not so easy in the city.

Up ahead, the other shoe is sitting at the top of the stairs, exactly where I left it. It's inches from Dave's door, steps from the pullout bed I can collapse into and the pile of blankets I can hide beneath. Eventually, I move toward the bottom step. The wood moans under my feet. My damp back itches but I don't dare scratch it. A toilet flushes on a higher floor and a door slams somewhere below. I wait for what seems like forever before taking the next step. There is a long way to go.

# Home

*Sixty days.* It's my first thought before opening my eyes after a restless night on Dave's pullout. And then: *Thirty to go.* I look at my watch and it's a few minutes past nine. I jump from the creaky pullout, hurry through my shower, get dressed, fold the mattress back into the couch, rearrange the cushions, and tidy up the place. I want to be up and out by the time Dave arrives. I don't want to be underfoot and, more than that, I don't want—not right now—to see him. I can't bear that look of worry on his face. Though we've been friends for years, the look belongs to someone more warden than friend. It says without saying a word, *Get sober and then we'll talk,* and I don't blame him. So I tiptoe down those wretched steps and leave for the day.

It's almost ten by the time I'm out of the building. I buy a cup of coffee from the closest bodega and wander around the neighborhood to get my bearings. None of it seems familiar. I've lived in New York for twelve years and I feel like I've never been here before. It's quiet and leafy and appears unimaginably expensive. Every shop is one I haven't seen before, every restaurant a place I can't afford. I eventually make my way toward the meeting to see Asa, as planned, and as I'm approaching 10th Street and Fifth Avenue I remember a deal I struck with Jack: never to step within a two-block radius of One Fifth. This rules out Washington Square Park, all of University Place and Sixth Avenue between 8th and 10th Streets, and Fifth Avenue south of 10th Street. I'm also not to go within a two-block radius of Sixth Avenue and Houston, where my old drug buddy Mark's apartment is and where much of my last drug use happened. The area around the now shut literary agency I co-owned, just north of Madison Square Park, is also off-limits. These places are what Jack calls triggers and I am to avoid them at all costs. For a moment I worry that the meeting where I'm joining Asa is off-limits, but then realize it sits on the 10th Street border, half a block east of Fifth. If it were one door south of 10th Street, I wouldn't be able to go.

I reach Fifth Avenue—the first time since coming home—
and as the old familiar Art Deco tower that is One Fifth
comes into view I feel like a ghost haunting my old life. How
many times did I rush down this street toward home, worrying that Noah had changed the locks? How many times did I
walk up Fifth toward the agency with a blistering hangover,
gutted from being up the night before? Standing on the same
pavement where I once walked with such agony I can't help
but wonder: *How was I that person? How did it go on for so
long?* I walk toward the meeting and begin to think I should
never have come back, that I should have accepted my sister
Kim's offer to live with her in Maine. How did I think it was
possible to be here? Every inch of this neighborhood carries
a memory of my life before. I look south, toward Washing-
ton Square Park, and I can see, just a few blocks away, the
two oversized green awnings of One Fifth jutting out over
the sidewalk. As clear as day I can see the corner windows
of the apartment where Noah and I lived for six years, where
Noah still lives. The last six weeks have passed in hospital rooms, rehab, and, last night, an unfamiliar apartment.
Everything that has happened—breaking up with Noah, everyone knowing I'm a crack addict, the end of my career,
the company gone, all the anger and disappointment—these
things have all registered, yes, but collectively and in the
abstract. This moment, however, is as concrete as the sidewalk I am standing on. This place before me—with shining

windows and green awnings flapping in the breeze—was home and now is not. I no longer belong here. From some far memory comes the doomy voice of my childhood piano teacher, who predicted, after too many hours spent attempting to teach my distracted, unpracticed self, that I would one day grow up to become a crack addict, just as the most notorious girl in my hometown had. *You'll have your come-uppance,* she forecast on more than one occasion, without a hint of doubt in her Irish brogue. *One day you'll have a rude awakening, and when you do it will take your breath away.* And so it has.

I turn onto the street where the meeting is and see a blond woman pushing a stroller toward me. It's Jane, an old friend of Noah's from Yale and the wife of a former client whom I haven't spoken to in many months. Jane's also a bestselling and highly respected author, and as she approaches I think, *Of all the people in the world who I could run into, why her?* As she looks up it occurs to me that she might not say a word, that she may just pass me by and pretend I'm not there. Of course she will. I'm a pariah now. That's what people do when they encounter a pariah. They don't see them.

Jane slows down, kick-locks the stroller, and steps toward me. Without a word, she gently grabs my arms, pulls me in, and kisses me on the cheek. Quick, without ceremony, over-before-it's-happened. She pats my shoulders, looks at me tenderly, and steps away. *Jane,* is all I manage to stammer before she's unlocked the stroller and is off again down the street.

It's 12:25 and I'm already late to meet Asa. I sprint toward the meeting, still bewildered by Jane's kindness. I see the research library where the meeting is held and go in. The security guard asks me to sign a sheet and tells me the meeting is on the fifth floor. *How does he know I'm going to the meeting?* I think, worried that I look as unbuckled as I feel. I scribble my name and the time, and hurry up the stairs. On the fifth floor there is a reading room with beautifully carved bookshelves and wide panes of glass that look out onto the planted terraces and curtained windows adorning the backs of town houses and apartment buildings on 11th Street. Something about the room feels familiar, tugs at an old memory, like a room from a house I knew in childhood, but I know I've never been here before. Midday light streams in from the windows. Before I look around for Asa I sit down, rest my chin against my chest, close my eyes, and exhale. The shaky alienation I felt on the street just minutes ago calms with each breath. I feel small but safe, and at the edge of tears. I look up and Asa is in the seat next to me. Perfect khakis, black Izod, pink belt, freckled everywhere. *Hi,* he says, smiling. *I wondered if you'd show.* His red hair, in the gushing light, glows like a halo. It's preposterous, I know this, but it really does. He puts his hand on my shoulder, this person I've known for less than twenty-four hours but who feels like my best friend in the world. He puts his hand on my shoulder, leans forward, and gives me a powerful hug. *You're a mess,* he says. *You're a mess and you're going to be just fine.*

# Speck in Streetscape

I'm lost in the West Village again. I've been at Dave's for almost a week and the streets west of Seventh Avenue are still hexed in some way that makes me always end up in front of the small park at the top of Horatio Street, or anywhere on Seventh Avenue south of 14th. It's raining. I'm on Jane Street. I know there's a coffee shop nearby, the one Jack and I went to between meetings on my first day back. I head what I think is west and recognize a little green banner at the end of the block. I'm splattered with rain but still basically dry by the time I get there. There is an advertisement for a pottery studio above the coffee shop sign but there is no pottery, not a trace of it, in the place. The owner is one of the most

*31*

beautiful men in New York (Jack and I had decided this last week) and also one of the meanest.

The small, low-ceilinged room is packed. Scruffy twenty-year-olds who look like they star in their own reality shows huddle into their laptops writing—what? screenplays? short stories? Are these the people who used to send me their manuscripts with letters that began with plot summaries? Why are they all so relentlessly attractive? No one moves from their seat and I realize I don't have any cash on me. There's no cash machine in the shop and the rain is pelting outside. *Can I help you?* the mean beauty snaps from behind jars overflowing with complicated cookies. His eyes, I notice, are green and gold and flash my way with nothing but contempt and impatience. *I'm waiting for someone,* I stutter, and as if he's been expecting this exact response he says, *Well, how about ordering something while you do that.*

Is this actually happening? Do I now have some scent or sign that lets people know that I'm down, I'm broke, banished, have few defenses, and can be kicked?

*Maybe* is all I come up with as I turn my back to him and pretend to make a phone call. Who can I call? I can't call Jack again. I've left three messages between last night and this morning already. I'm seeing Asa at a meeting in a church uptown later and, as I have with Jack, I've left too many voice mails to leave another. I can feel the barista's eyes flashing anger at my back. I dial fake random numbers and say *hey* in the most casual, I-have-dozens-of-friends-happy-to-hear-from-me kind of way. I perform one half of an intimate conversation and worry that at any second this guy is going to escort me out the door and into the rain. I fib a quick *See you later,* flip the phone shut, turn around, and sure enough, the pretty prick is leaning against the counter, arms crossed, with a look on his face that can only be described as disgust.

I can't take another second so I leave. The rain is coming down in sheets and the streets are empty. I walk to the end of the block and head what I think is east. It's 3:30, I've already been to my gym (the year's membership has luckily been paid) and two meetings, but have two hours to kill before I can go back to Dave's place before meeting Asa later. I stumble onto Hudson and realize I've gone west. Barnes & Noble in Union Square is the only place I can think of going where I can disappear for a few hours without it being obvious that

I have nowhere else to go. It's at least a twenty-minute walk, but I turn around anyway and head back toward Jane. The rain is colder than it was before, pushier. I find a broken umbrella sticking out of a Dumpster and for a few blocks agree to a fiction that it's actually keeping me dry. There is a moment—water sloshing from my shoes, T-shirt plastered to my chest, rain dripping from the brim of my NYC Parks Department cap—when I stop and look around. I have no idea where I am. Not one building or business looks familiar. I've gone east past Jane and what I thought was north. I don't see any street signs. Am I anywhere? I wonder. Do I even exist anymore? I've lost all sense of direction and feel as if the rain is about to blast me into a billion microscopic particles. I've never felt so small. I start calling people— Dave, Jack, Kim, Jean, Asa—and reach only outgoing voice mail messages. I have nothing to say so I hang up each time and dial the next number. I imagine them all safe in their warm, dry offices and apartments, surrounded by colleagues, pets, ringing phones, and freshly brewed coffee. I think of the agency, now gone, and the night only months ago when I showed up and the locks had been changed. How on the other side of that locked door sat furniture that Kate and I had picked out and carried from a store on Park Avenue South. After that night, I would never see that office again. I stop dialing the phone, which is now slick with rainwater and very likely to be broken soon.

I've been back for five days, have sixty-four days sober, and with ninety days almost in sight I don't know how, on the other side of it, I'll be able to hold things together, how I'll stay in the city. Jack's slogans and Asa's assurances aren't helping. There is no money coming in, it's all going out, the bills are mounting, and I have to find an apartment in the next week before Dave throws me out. I feel like one of the street urchins Dickens describes in his books. Like little Jo in *Bleak House*, who dies of something bronchial and grim like consumption once his use to the world has expired. Mine has too. Like this ridiculous umbrella, whatever fantasy I had of being OK, of making my way back in a city of overachieving winners, is now quite obviously a figment, a pathetic shield against an overwhelming truth. It's over. I'm a Dickensian speck in a city that no longer has use for me. I had my time here and in that time got lucky, played my cards well for a while, and then very badly.

I put the umbrella down, let the rain drench any remaining patches of dry clothing and skin, put my face to the sky and think, and then say, *OK*. The city disappears around me and there are only the elements. Wind and water, freezing and clean. *OK*, I say again, not really understanding what it is I am agreeing to, what it is precisely I am accepting. But I am accepting something. The truth of my circumstances?

The reality I have until now avoided? It's much worse than I imagined and also somehow better. Is this the bottom I hear people refer to in meetings? The grim despair that makes change possible?

I walk without any sense of direction. At this point I don't care where I go. I'll walk until five, get soaked until Dave has left the studio. There is no one on the sidewalks, no cars on the streets. The maze of the West Village is empty. Thunderclaps and wild sheets of rain slap against the asphalt. Had I ever heard thunder in New York? Was it like everything else that I took for granted—these streets, the cost of things, love—and can only now recognize?

Up ahead an awning sticks out over a dry patch of sidewalk and I quickly walk toward it and duck under. It's a small real estate agency and in the window there are photographs of apartments. I remember when Noah and I would stand in front of windows like this one and gawk at the high-ceilinged, new-kitchened beauties. Looking at these shiny, meticulous spaces now only reminds me that I don't have my own and the one I'll end up in—should I end up in one at all—will not be like these.

The wind starts blowing the rain horizontally and the awning no longer provides protection. A sudden squall of rain explodes against the window, the awning, the drenched length of me, and in a panic I jump inside the real estate agency. Dripping wet, I close the door, and as I do four people sitting at desks look up and say hello in unison. I tell them I'm looking for an apartment to rent, which is true, though I have no plan to go through an agency and pay the outrageous broker's fee that is usually at least two months' rent. Still, the little place is warm and dry and I have time to kill. I tell them that I'm taking a sabbatical from work and looking for a cheaper place to rent. Computers flutter to life, images of apartments with rental statistics shine from screens, and one of the agents, a middle-aged bald man, says he knows of a great studio with a terrace that's about to come on the market. Turns out it's just a few blocks from here and he could get me in tomorrow at noon before anyone else sees it. *Sure,* I say, with no intention at all of showing up. We exchange numbers, he gives me the address where I am to meet him the next day, and after a round of good-byes I'm back on the street.

I keep the little slip of paper in my pocket through the meeting that night and miraculously it finds its way into my pants the next day. I pull it from my front pocket around 11:30 that morning and think of the bald guy showing up at the building and me nowhere to be found. It seems like something I might have done before and felt guilty about. Something I would have cringed over later as I downed vodka after vodka until I forgot it altogether. So I go meet the guy in front of the building at 15th Street and Seventh Avenue. When I get there I realize this is the block where I lived when I first met Noah. The block where the apartment I owned when I was twenty-five is and where my girlfriend Nell and I lived for almost three years. I always felt more comfortable on this street than I did at One Fifth, and as I look down the block I see that it hasn't changed much. It's still a mix of rent-controlled mid-century apartment buildings, older tenements, hair salons, and renovated brownstones. I can't remember the last time I was here. I sold the apartment—the second floor of a carriage house at the back of a courtyard—years ago so I'd have money once we started the literary agency, but after that I don't think I ever came back.

I meet the bald guy in the small lobby and we go up to the seventeenth floor. As he unlocks the door to the apartment, I have a strong feeling of déjà vu, not unlike the feeling I had that first day at the Library meeting. We walk into the short hallway and before we've reached the one and only room, before I've seen the small terrace that looks out over the city, to the Empire State Building and beyond, before I see the little kitchen with space enough for a desk, and the simple black-and-white-tiled bathroom, and before I worry where I'll find the money for the first and last months' rent, the deposit, and the broker's fee, before any of this, words come out of my mouth, and as I say them I know they're true: *This is it. I'm home.*

# Re-entry

Seventy-four days. Sixteen to go. First morning waking up in the apartment on 15th Street. I stay up until midnight the night before and, from my bed, watch the lights of the Empire State Building click off. I can almost hear the old skyscraper sigh as it goes dark, as if exhausted from the long day. I haven't unpacked or set the place up yet, but I've moved my things in from One Fifth. Noah and I agree I should move out without him around, so three days before I move out of Dave's (and with permission from Jack to cross into the trigger zone), I go. I ask my friend Cy if she'll come with me and she agrees. I ask her for several reasons. One, she's been up to White Plains a few times and has been supportive. Two, she's worked as a counselor for people diagnosed with HIV, AIDS, and other fatal illnesses since the eighties and very little makes her blink. Three, she's drop-dead gorgeous, unusually chic, and, well, the woman can enter a building. It comforts me somewhat that she will be at my side, like a glamorous force field, as I re-enter for the first time the building I left on a stretcher. She meets me in front of One Fifth, looking like she always does, thank God, hooks her arm in mine, and says, *OK, kid, let's get this over with*. I practically hide behind her as we enter. Even though Noah arranges for keys to be left at the front desk, and even with Cy at my side, I'm afraid they won't let me in. It's been two months since I collapsed through these same doors, unable to stand up, begging for a key. Two months since the ambu-lance drove me away to Lenox Hill.

José, one of the doormen, is at the desk and the moment he sees me says, with exaggerated kindness and what I can't help but suspect is sarcasm, *Noah has left you keys.* How many times did José buzz up one of my dealers or watch me come in the door with shady characters I'd picked up in Washing-ton Square Park when Noah was away? He can be sarcastic all he wants, I think, and suddenly wonder how many other people in the building carried on the way I had. Anyone? Many? In rehab and in the meetings I've heard dozens of sto-ries like mine—on-the-surface successful people carrying on what look like respectable lives in buildings like this one, who at night turned into drug-addled zombies, buzzing up drug-dealing-and-using vampires from their lobbies. Maybe I wasn't the only one at One Fifth living such a messy life. Maybe I wasn't anything out of the ordinary. As much as I want to believe this, the wary and pitying look in José's eyes suggests otherwise.

Cy and I get in the elevator and get off on the sixth floor. The hallway is just as it was, just a hallway. Indifferent, a little stuffy with its green-and-gold-striped walls and beige corporate carpeting. The new locks in the door are still shiny, and as we enter the apartment, Benny is right away at our feet—meowing and purring and then, unlike her, immediately slinking away, out of sight. She disappears into the den and only later creeps to the edge of the bedroom while I'm packing my clothes into duffel bags. *Join the club,* I say to her as she eyes me doubtfully from across the room and keeps her distance.

It will take two and a half days to get all my stuff, including the cat, out of Noah's and over to 15th Street. Cy doesn't come back the next days but it's OK. I race through the place taking clothes from drawers, jackets and shoes from closets, and pulling books off the shelves Noah and I had built when we first moved in. The ones we found the design for in a book called *Living with Books*. We bought a pile of similar books and over dinner one night at L'Acajou pored over the glossy pages until we found a simple design that fit the place. Did I get drunk that night? I wonder painfully. Pulling my books from the shelves and shoving them into cardboard boxes, I cringe with regret and wish that I could go back in time and do it all differently. But even if I could, would I be able to keep from drinking? Keep from sneaking into the bathroom and calling a dealer? Even within spitting distance of ninety days I'm not so sure.

I snoop for signs of a new love. I'm queasy with jealousy, even though I ended our relationship at the strong recommendation of my counselor in rehab, my sister, and several close friends who all urged me to get sober on my own, away from what each described in one way or another as a codependent dynamic of addict and enabler that Noah and I had, it seems, perfected. My desperation and need of their support were and are so great that I didn't question them and agreed. Noah is angry with me at first, but a counselor from the rehab calls and explains and asks him to give me the space I need to get healthy. I have not seen him for over two months, and our only contact has been crisp and spare and specific to the details of my moving out. Rarely does an hour go by when I don't question the decision to break up, doubt that it's the right choice. But something more than the advice of others keeps me from changing my mind, something beyond logic or want that keeps me from calling Noah and running back into his arms.

In between packing boxes and duffel bags, I check the caller ID box for unfamiliar and frequently appearing phone numbers (too many to form any conclusions); sift through the bedside table drawers for evidence of sex—lubricant, condoms—and find nothing; frisk Noah's gray Helmut Lang blazer and the pockets of his gray snap-front jacket and, again, nothing. Just lighters and cigarettes, which it's clear he's now taken up again, openly. I'd been a tyrant about smoking when we were together, which now seems just as ironic and hypocritical as it was.

On the last day, once everything is packed and ready to go, I sit in the corner window of the living room and finger the beige and brown animal print fabric on the window seat. There is a small square pillow made with the same fabric leaning against the window and I wonder if I should take it with me. The fabric came from a store in Islington, in Lon-

don, where we spent four or five weekends in an apartment
I split the rent on in my twenties. Buying that fabric, having that window seat cushion and pillow made, seemed, at
twenty-seven, like the most adult, most worldly thing one
could do. I laugh out loud at my younger, now faraway self
and am amused for a brief flash before the tight fist of grief
returns. I watch the early evening lights blink on up lower
Fifth Avenue and the white headlights rush toward me. How
many times had I sat here? And in what states—furious,
ashamed, worried, high, hopeful, hating, drunk, arrogant,
panicked, exhausted, in love? I sit for a few more minutes
and remember as much as I can before I go. I leave the pillow
behind.

Several nights later, Dave organizes tickets to go to the
opera. I think but am not sure we see *Aida* that night. I
remember it was long and one of the older Zeffirelli pro-
ductions at the Met. We eat dinner in the overpriced, still
glamorous restaurant on the Grand Tier level of the building. Starters and main course during the first intermission
and dessert and coffee during the second. Dave's seats at
the opera are good ones—center Grand Tier, which is
the second balcony, second row, in the middle—and the
people seated around us all look like longtime operagoers,
dressed nicely, not extravagantly like the tourists in the or-

chestra section. I can't help but think everyone here has been sitting in these seats since they were teenagers, have seen these operas hundreds of times, and are quite alert to the polluting presence of anyone who has not. Having spent the day at the 12:30 and two o'clock Library meetings, and the afternoon sitting in Union Square with Asa, telling him about some of the grittier details of the double life I lived as an addict, I find that this refined eveningscape does not feel comfortable.

Over dinner, Dave keeps talk within the firm boundaries of opera, his family, and popular culture. Only once does he ask how things are going and I am careful not to sound too positive or too discouraged. I don't actually say, *One day at a time,* but I might as well. I am like a careful apprentice with a benevolent but stern mentor. Aware at every second that I am lucky to be given any time at all in light of his many kindnesses—the pickup and drop-off at rehab, the use of the writing studio on Charles Street, all the phone calls and e-mails he's had to field from concerned and angry people who became aware that he was in contact with me after I disappeared months ago. I tread carefully and wonder if we'll ever be at ease with each other again.

Once the opera is over we take a cab downtown. I'm grateful
he directs the driver to my address first and then his own,
as I know my days of paying for cab rides are over. We say
our good-byes and I head into my building for what will be
my second night there. I get into the elevator, which—despite the fact that the apartment is relatively cheap and the
building is all rentals—has an elevator man. The one on
duty now is not one I've seen before, so I tell him to go
to seventeen. He says, *OK, boss,* in an accent that I think
must be either Croatian or Georgian. I get to my apartment
and notice two large paper shopping bags hanging from the
doorknob. When I see the quiche boxes from Eli's bakery
jutting out from one of the bags, I know they're from Jean.
There is a card taped to a handle and on it my name is
scrawled in Jean's inimitably looping and jagged cursive. Inside it reads, *Welcome to your new home and your new life.
With so much love, Jean.* I open the door and unpack the bags,
which are filled with quiches and salads and roasted meats.
Some of the food is from Eli's bakery, some from Zabar's,
and some made by Jean's chef, Paul. There are even delicate
Austrian chocolates from the Neue Gallerie. After I put the
food away, I stand in front of the now full refrigerator and
shout, *THANK YOU, JEAN!* I realize, with relief and a little
gust of confidence, that I don't have to buy food for at least a
week.

I go out to the terrace. It's a crisp spring night and the lights of the city are dancing. It's after midnight, so I can make out only the ghosty outline of the now dark Empire State Building. I'm relieved to be away from Dave, away from what I imagine to be his nervous scrutiny. I think about his writing studio on Charles Street—the creaky steps, the downstairs neighbor poised to pounce at the slightest hint of nefarious activity. I think of the entire precarious time there and remember how during the first afternoon, within minutes of Dave's leaving, I'd been consumed with the desire to get high. How lucky I didn't, I think. What a miracle the craving passed. The city blinks its light, police sirens sound, faint music from another apartment comes and goes with the breeze. And then, just as it had that afternoon, the old craving returns. How do I describe it? It's like skin that feels perfectly fine one moment and then is ablaze with an itch the next. It looks the same: skin—harmless, unfettered skin. But all at once it's screaming to be ravaged with fingernails and rubbed raw.

I look back into the apartment through the small square window in the door and think, *There is nothing and no one to stop me.* I can get high in this apartment, which is mine alone, and no one is coming home or arriving in the morning. I then look down at the scattered traffic on Seventh Avenue and think, *If all else fails there are seventeen floors and a hard sidewalk.* I know I should call Jack. Or Asa. Or one of the dozen numbers that are now in my phone from people at The Library and other meetings. *CALL SOMEONE!* I say out loud, but even as I say the words I know it's too late. My mind whizzes with ways to get drugs. Since Jack made me get a new cell phone, I don't have Happy's or Rico's numbers. And I can't remember them. Then it occurs to me: Mark's place on Houston and Sixth. He's always using and always up. It's midweek and before 1:00 a.m. If he doesn't already have drugs in the apartment he can easily get some. Better to go there than to call Happy or Rico anyway, since I owe them each a thousand dollars.

I go. Out the door, down the elevator, and onto Seventh Avenue, where I quickly duck into a bodega and head to the cash machine. I have less than two hundred dollars in my checking account, but I also have three credit cards with separate limits for cash advances. I dimly remember being asked to set a PIN code for at least one. I am practically dancing as I scour my wallet for credit cards. I try one and use the PIN for my regular cash card and it doesn't work. I try another and get the same result. I try the third, and again no luck. So I go back to the first and play around with a few combinations of the PIN code for my cash card.

I replace the last two numbers with zeros and BINGO!!!—
it works. I advance four hundred dollars and am electric
with the anticipation of getting high. It's been so long. I
rush out onto Seventh Avenue and a cab immediately pulls
up. I step in and realize that at some point, either on the
terrace or just after, I have left the world I had been living
in and entered another—or rather re-entered the one that
had been waiting.

I tell the cabdriver the address and I think I hear him say,
*Didn't take long.* Right away, I ask him what he just said and
he responds calmly, in a Jamaican accent, *Nothing my friend,
nothing.* We're at Mark's in a few minutes and to my surprise
the meter registers a fare, which he is clearly waiting for. I
pay and he mumbles something which I hear as *Be God,* but
figure he means *Be good.*

I'm at the door. The same door I've stood at dozens and
dozens of times. Looking at the same buzzer and hoping
the same hope: that Mark is home and that Mark has drugs.
Whatever hesitation struggled against desire on the terrace
less than an hour before is now gone. I am giddy and antsy
and shuffling before the door as if something wonderful is
waiting on the other side. Nothing of the past months, noth-

ing of the ruin and upset my using has caused, figures into this moment. Or if it does, it's a dim unpleasantness that, along with every other worry, is being escaped. The world and its woe exist on this side of the door, where I am now; the place to hide from it all is on the other, where I'm going. I press the button and in seconds hear Mark's voice, metallic and loud through the intercom. *Who is it?* he squawks, and before I say my name the door is buzzing open.

# One Day

It's early afternoon, two days after showing up at Mark's apartment, when I return home. Benny hasn't been fed for almost three days, and when I open the door she is meowing desperately. I immediately open a fresh can of cat food, put water in her bone-dry dish, and try to pet her, but she bites at my hands and skitters away. I plug in my cell phone, which is dead and I know will be full of messages—from Jack, Asa, Kim, Jean, Dave. I'm starving and I take one of the quiches from the refrigerator and eat the entire thing. I've purchased Tylenol PM from the bodega downstairs and take a handful to cushion the crash. I wish I had vodka or beer or some kind of alcohol, but even after forty-eight hours of crack and vodka at Mark's the idea of bringing booze into

this apartment seems out of bounds. So the Tylenol PM will
have to do. Once the phone is charged I listen to the messages: three from Kim—one more worried than the next—
two from Dave, whom Kim has called because she has not
heard from me, none from Jack, two from Asa, and one from
Polly.


Polly is a few years younger than I am, lives with her twin
sister, Heather, who is the bartender at an Irish tavern in the
West Village that serves burgers and steaks and chicken pot
pies. Heather and Polly are coke addicts. Polly is trying to
get sober, Heather is not.


Polly has six or seven days clean. I met her at that first meeting at The Library with Asa. When I raised my hand that
day, as Jack had insisted I do, and said I had sixty days, Polly
waved to me from across the room and smiled while everyone else clapped. Later, Polly raised her hand and shared that
she was afraid Heather would overdose and that it had been
difficult to put together more than a few days clean when
their dealer was still coming in and out of the apartment at all
hours.

One of the most frightening things Polly said that day was that she once had six years sober. She and Heather got sober after college and then, four years ago, after graduate school and a few broken hearts between them, they moved in together. Three years later, they both relapsed. Neither had gone more than a week since without getting high.

Polly lost her job as a schoolteacher six months ago and walks dogs to pay the few hundred dollars that is her portion of the rent-controlled apartment they share on St. Mark's Place. Polly is my height, very thin, and is often wearing sweatpants and T-shirts that don't look washed. Her hair is shoulder length, dirty blond, and greasy, and she reeks of cigarette smoke. She has a dog named Essie—a fat, mid-sized gray-and-white mutt she walks up and down the side streets of the East Village while she chain-smokes. Her clothes are usually covered in dog hair.

My first response to Polly when she smiled at me at The Library was *Fuck, I hope she doesn't want to talk after the meeting;* but when she described—plainly, clearly—how desperate she was not to use again but feared she would, there was a moment when I confused the words she was saying with the words I was thinking, believed momentarily that they were coming from inside my head and not from across the room. I looked again at this skeletal, disheveled, unwashed mess, and as she spoke I got very still because everything she was relating was something I had felt before and in precisely the same way. When the meeting ended, I was the one to chase after her, down the stairs and into the street, to ask for her phone number.

Polly's voice mail message is short and sweet: *Hey, I didn't see you in the meeting yesterday or today. What's up? Call me.* I do. She picks up on the first ring and says in a playful, school-teacher tone, *Billy boy, did you relapse?* I mumble in response some kind of yes. She laughs. She actually laughs, and says, *Get to a meeting, don't sit on the pity pot, just get to a meeting. Don't make a big deal out of it, just get back on the beam. And call your sponsor.* I listen to Polly like I'm listening to someone telling me how to defuse a bomb strapped to my ankle. *OK, OK,* I say and agree to call her later that night.

It's Thursday evening and I've already missed two meetings at The Library. I sit on my bed and look out the window toward the building that used to be Barneys but is now, vaguely and in ways that don't make sense to me, a museum for Tibetan culture. Things change, things stay the same, but

I remain an addict. I think about one of the writers I represented whose book is now on the bestseller list and being smothered in acclaim. She has kept in touch, came to rehab once for a walk, and gave me the first signed copy of the book, but she is gone now and my professional relationship to her work a thing of the past. As with Kate and Noah, and even friends like Dave and Jean, I can only envision her happiness and success and my lack of both. I don't imagine that within any of their lives there is strife or fear or regret or sadness. When I have tried to explain this to Jack, he interrupts me and says, *ENOUGH SELF-PITY!* which of course I find humiliating. I also find it strange that with all the people who have left me messages on my cell phone, Jack is not one of them. I'm sure Kim called him — she's had his number since I was in the hospital.

As the Tylenol PM begins to kick in, I start thinking about Jack's patronizing phrases, his dismissive accusations of self-pity, and how he never just listens to what I'm feeling, what I'm going through. If not him, then who? He's my sponsor, isn't he? I think about going back to Mark's, but I know there won't be any more drugs there until evening when he can call Happy or Rico. Mark agreed not to tell Happy that I was in the bedroom when he came with the drugs two nights ago, because of the money I owe him. I wonder if Mark kept his word or instead tipped him off that I'm back in town. Worry about Happy mingles with my rising resentment toward Jack, and in a burst of frustration I pick up the lamp next to my bed and throw it against a wall. The light bulb shatters but the small wooden base remains intact. Next to the wall where I've thrown the lamp I see a meeting book. Reluctantly, I pick it up to see if there is a mid-afternoon meeting nearby. I can't bear to call anyone else back and have no idea what I will say when I eventually do. I flip through the meeting book and see one starting in ten minutes a few blocks away at the gay and lesbian center. I go.

The meeting is small, gloomy, and filled with mostly middle-aged gay men who look sick. I'm on the end of two days smoking crack and guzzling vodka with no food or sleep, so I don't look so hot either. The meeting is a round robin format where everyone is expected to talk once the speaker has qualified, which means he describes, in ten to thirty minutes, what it was like when he used, how he got sober, and what it's like now. I make it through the first ten minutes of the speaker's qualification and I can't bear the idea of talking, of having to admit I've just relapsed; and I don't want these guys crowding me after the meeting with their numbers and their understanding faces. I want to leave, so I do.

I call Polly from the street and she picks up right away. *Did you go to a meeting and say that you've relapsed?* she snaps without salutation and I lie and say yes. *Which one?* she asks doubtfully and I tell her. *Did you call your sponsor?* I lie again and say yes. *So what are you going to do now?* she asks, and the truth is I have no idea. I tell her so and she says, *Well, let's talk.* I don't remember everything we talked about that night, but I do remember her telling me a story of getting drunk on a flight to Dallas, where, once she landed, she blew off the rehearsal dinner for a wedding she was supposed to be a bridesmaid in to go looking for an ex-boyfriend. She hit a bar on the way and ended up walking in traffic on a freeway outside the city and getting arrested. I tell her how I was—just three months earlier—thrown off a flight to Berlin because I was convinced the plane was crawling with DEA agents and said something bizarre to the flight attendant. We talk and trade war stories, and I walk west on 15th Street, north on Eighth Avenue, east on 16th Street, south on Seventh Avenue, west on 15th, completing the loop around the block again and again and again. Polly keeps me on the phone a long time, and I remember several times thinking that the dealers will be back in business soon and maybe I should get off the phone and go over to Mark's. But I stay on the phone, walk in circles until I'm exhausted, and, finally, go home.

I call Kim that night. Dave and Jean and Asa, too. The call with Dave lasts less than ten seconds and he says, *Good luck, call Kim.* It's clear he's had it and that I am not his problem anymore. Kim is similarly short with me. I leave a message for Jean on her answering machine that I'm OK and will speak with her in the morning. Asa and I talk. As with Polly, we stay on for a long time. Long enough for me to fall asleep, because I wake up at four or five in the morning with all the lights on and my cell phone pressed between my ear and the pillow. I get up to turn off the lights and find Benny asleep next to the door. I want to pet her, tell her how sorry I am for leaving her alone without food for over two days, but I'm afraid she'll bite me again, so I leave her alone and go back to bed.

It's after one o'clock when I wake up the next day. It's Friday and I've missed the 12:30 meeting at The Library, but I make coffee, eat a bowl of granola, shower, dress, and get out the door to make the two o'clock. Polly and Asa are both there when I walk in but I don't recognize anyone else. *C'mere, Crackhead,* Polly says and pats the seat next to her. She is wearing what looks like pajama bottoms. Asa, freckled and immaculate in his usual uniform of tight Izod, jeans, and colored belt, sits on my other side. I've never been so happy to see anyone as I am these two.

The meeting begins. There are two speakers—one with just over a year sober and the other with decades—who talk about early sobriety and the first ninety days. Of all days I should be listening, but I can't stop thinking about the four-hundred-dollar cash advance I put on my credit card to buy drugs. I start thinking about how much money I have left on that card and the others. I tally up ten grand or so and begin to imagine how I could put together a war chest of drugs for one last bender and then make use of the seventeenth-floor balcony off my apartment. No pills this time, no chance of failing again. Polly rubs the back of my neck and I can smell the cigarette smoke coming off her clothes. The speakers go on speaking, a hat gets passed and fills up with dollars, people raise their hands and announce their day counts—twenty-four, eighty-eight, thirty. People clap. Polly raises her hand and says nine or ten or something in that range. More clapping. She pinches my leg, I raise my hand. *One day,* I say, and the place explodes.

The meeting ends and as it breaks up six or seven people approach me, give me their numbers, and tell me to call any-time. I notice a short, thin, dark-haired girl wearing overalls and a striped cardigan whom I think I know from some-where. I'm pretty sure it's the on-again, off-again girlfriend of Noah's screenwriting partner, but I can't think of her name. She disappears through the door and up the stairs before I can remember.

I go with Polly to the dog run in Union Square Park and watch Essie get humped by the smallest dog I've ever seen. She wanders slowly around the narrow dirt yard, but her suitor keeps pace, bouncing from behind on brittle twig-thin legs. Polly and I drink coffee and the afternoon slips by. She tells me about having been a competitive swimmer in college and, years later, getting drunk on beer in the morning before going to work teaching elementary school kids. *Here we are, Crackhead,* she says, gesturing with her right hand toward the dog run, and then, like a wise sober owl, says, *Exactly where we're supposed to be.*

Three days later I don't see Polly at the 12:30 or two o'clock meetings at The Library. She doesn't show up to the Tuesday meeting either. She doesn't return my calls, and the few people we have in common haven't seen or heard from her since last Friday. Despite Jack's warnings that I should keep my distance and not chase after her, I hang out in front of the building where she and Heather live. She never appears. Finally, on Wednesday, she shows up at the two o'clock meeting, late, and sits toward the back. I try to catch her eye but she stares into her lap. She looks even more unkempt and ragged than usual and after the speaker finishes qualifying, she raises the same hand she used six days before to gesture grandly toward the dog run, Union Square, our lives. *I'm Polly,* she mutters. *I have one day.*

# The Rooms

I have eight days now and Polly has three. The last few days we've met at the 12:30, stayed for the two o'clock, and each time ended up at the dog run. I'm getting used to the dog run smells of piss and shit and am no longer worried that someone I know will see me. The same people are usually there. A few old ladies, several professional dog walkers like Polly, who come with dozens of cool-tempered, strangely obedient dogs on leashes. And then there are the young guys in tracksuits, expensive ones like my friend Lotto's. We met in the rehab Noah and Kate sent me to in Oregon last year after they organized an intervention with Dave and Kim. Lotto's a rich kid from New York and at the age of twenty-two has been to ten or eleven rehabs and two therapeutic boarding schools, something I didn't know existed before meeting him. He wears tracksuits—either Adidas brand or the shiny plush kind with fancy zippers and logos, the ones that look like they were purchased at expensive resorts. According to the last text he sent me, Lotto's at the Betty Ford Center in California, already having relapsed two or three times since returning to New York from Oregon. These guys in the dog park remind me of him, just older, twenty-seven, twenty-eight, maybe thirty. I imagine they do coke all night and stumble out in the afternoons to let their dogs go to the bathroom. With bloodshot eyes and jumbo coffee containers from Dean & Deluca and Starbucks, they text and call from their cell phones and I imagine them scoring bags of drugs for the coming night. I wonder who lives like this— expensive dogs, good haircuts, new running shoes, worked- out bodies, fancy phones, tracksuits. Who other than people like me and Polly who've wiped out and are getting sober can dawdle in a dog run at three o'clock on a weekday af- ternoon? Dealers? None of my dealers were ever white. But that doesn't mean that these guys aren't dealing. Maybe they're slightly older Lottos with families who've cut them off, so they deal drugs to keep using. The lifespan of this kind of dealer/user/aging rich kid must be short, I think, as I watch them retreat to the far benches of the dog run and grumble into their phones. I try to remember war stories from the meetings, or what Polly and Asa and lately I refer to as *the rooms,* to align with this profile but come up with nothing.

My mind dances through these possibilities but I don't share them with Polly for fear the speculation about dealers and using will trigger her. We talk a lot about Heather, how she's starting to shoot coke with needles, is missing work and being warned. *She's going to lose her job, get arrested, or die,* Polly says as she exhales a giant plume of cigarette smoke. *And every time I turn around there's a dealer in the living room and a bag of coke on the coffee table.* I offer, careful not to be too pushy, to help Polly look for a rehab or move her to a new apartment—at least until she has ninety days—but Polly's not ready. She says she'll take me up on either offer if it ever seems necessary or gets too bad at home.


We don't usually stay in the dog run longer than forty-five minutes, so on most days I'm back in my apartment for at least the last half of *The Oprah Winfrey Show.* In the last few episodes there has been little in the way of redemption stories. Instead, there is lots of shopping and *THINGS I LOVE,* like pies and perfumes, and accessories. Still, I'm transfixed by the show, which, up until now, I'd never really watched. I'm tempted to, but don't, rush Polly out of the dog run so I can catch as much of the show as possible. Somehow the four o'clock airing feels like an occasion, has the fizzy energy of watching the Academy Awards or the Grammys. There is a sense that the rest of the world is tuning in, and even though the show is taped, it feels live, as if Oprah is revealing something terribly important each day that her audience, which seems like everyone, absolutely must know. Even something as trivial as the best brownie in New England gets the royal treatment, or the doughnut that is *OUT OF THIS WORLD,* which she'll shout about loudly and with mannish glee. Whatever it is she's shouting about, I'm there. And I'm sorry it's over when it is. There are more commercials in the second half hour, so my glimpses of the show are skimpy and I'm cranky it doesn't start later. The first time I get back to the apartment by four o'clock, I can't believe how long the show goes on without a commercial break at the beginning.

Later that year, in the fall, Oprah picks a book about drug addiction for her book club. The book came out a few years before and, at the time, I started to read it but stopped. I'm not sure exactly why I stopped—probably because I had too much reading and editing to do for work—but I didn't make it past the first twenty or so pages, which I barely remember. I do remember thinking it had a macho arrogance but that the writing—vivid, swift, fresh—was very good. That's all. This was during a period when I was struggling—and not successfully—to control my drug use and my drinking. No one but Noah knew I smoked crack. But this guy, this author, said he smoked crack, too, and I was fascinated that he was able to get sober. I read many of the interviews with him when the book was first published, pored over the articles where he talked about rehab, what they tried to teach him there, the tools for recovery they suggested he use—the Twelve Steps, the support of other alcoholics and addicts—and how he rejected it all and relied on his own willpower to quit. Over the years, Noah had begged me to go to rehab, but like this guy I didn't think I needed what they had. In all of his interviews and later, on *Oprah,* he described confidently, persuasively, how he realized he could quit on his own and he didn't, and still doesn't, need a program of recovery. It was all very appealing, what he described, and the willpower he cited appeared to be incredibly strong. He simply chose to stop drinking and drugging because, he said, he knew if he didn't he would die. Back when the book first came out, when I first heard what he had to say about recovery, it sounded perfectly logical, and I strongly identified with the belief that the usual routes of rehab, Twelve Steps groups, and other fellowships of recovery were not for everyone. Not for this guy. Not for me. I just hadn't made the choice yet, I reasoned then, and figured that when I finally did decide to stop, I would, like this guy, be able to.

Now, after losing most everything, going to rehab twice, and only eight days from my last relapse, I cannot identify with him at all. What he describes seems superhuman. Why is it so easy for some people? I wonder. It must be that I'm made of lesser matter, I decide, and continue to believe that, later, when I see Oprah heap praise on him for being so strong. When I see the show featuring the author that fall, I am still going to three meetings a day, have no job or other obligations, and watch people in the same situation relapsing as I did again and again and again. And this guy, well, he just chose to stop using. By his own account, he doesn't go to meetings, certainly not three a day. He's like those people who don't have to work out to have perfect bodies. I'd give anything to be one of those people. Pizza, ice cream, bowls and bowls of granola, and six-pack abs. No meetings, no sponsor, no fellowship and—poof!—long-term sobriety. But it's still April and that author won't appear on the *Oprah* show until September. The book is already a big success before Oprah picks it for her book club, and from time to time over that spring and summer I hear people who don't want to go to meetings or work with a sponsor use the book as an example of how it's possible to stay clean on one's own, without help, through sheer willpower.

Eight days sober and finishing my fourth bowl of granola as the *Oprah* show ends, my willpower isn't feeling so formidable. I think about skipping the six o'clock at the Meeting House—a Library-like evening meeting I go to at the end of most weekdays—and begin to think about going down to Mark's to get high. It's less than a moment between fleeting thought and full-blown fantasy, barely a second before becoming a fully articulated obsessive vision of getting to Mark's, calling a dealer, loading a pipe, and inhaling that first hit. My phone starts ringing—it's my father—and as I hear the phone ring a few more times and let the call go to voice mail, the spell is broken long enough for me to bolt out the door toward the Meeting House a few blocks away. The meeting doesn't start for an hour, so I make phone calls to Kim, Polly, and Jack until the doors are unlocked. I cannot understand why I still want to use. Cannot understand why I have so little defense against picking up once the idea pops into my head. I know the consequences, know it will devolve into paranoid desperation almost as soon as it begins, but smoking crack still seems like a good idea. *It's insane,* I think, and not for the first time. I'm insane. Am I one of those people in the rooms whom I hear others talk about, who quite literally cannot get sober—one of those cases who are incapable of being honest with themselves? And what does honesty with oneself have to do with anything?

The doors are still locked and I cross the street so I don't seem as desperate as I am. *What am I doing wrong?* I think. I'm getting sober the way Jack has told me to: I go to as many meetings as I can, call him every day, do what he says, and when in doubt or I can't reach him, I call other addicts and alcoholics in recovery. Which is what I'm doing right now. BUT NOBODY IS PICKING UP THEIR FUCKING PHONE! I lean against a building across from the Meeting House, try to calm down, and think back over the last few weeks. In a short time my days have become predictable: wake up, feed Benny, gym; 12:30 Library meeting, which I arrive at early because it's much more crowded than the one at two o'clock; a short break to get a coffee and rush back to the same seat for the two o'clock meeting. The 12:30 meeting—filled with well-dressed nine-to-five types wedging a lunch hour meeting into their workday—has a much higher wattage than the two o'clock, which is smaller and attended by a mix of out-of-work and newly sober day counters, artists, actors, writers, evening-shift waiters, and others with flexible schedules. Some of the most articulate, charismatic, persuasive people I have ever encountered are in the 12:30 meeting. The only speaking I do there is to share my day count. The same people tend to be encouraging afterward: Rafe, one of the most visible, is one. He's super-sober, super-visible, and super-gay. *Good to see you, Bill, keep coming back,* he'll say in his particular intonation, with a knowing emphasis on the word *Bill*. There is also Madge, an ex–Max's Kansas City intellectual rock chick with an eye patch, a Jane-Fonda-in-*Klute* shag haircut, and a sandpaper and gravel voice shaped as much by Upper East Side, Martha's Vineyard privilege as it is by drugs and thousands of hours logged in the smoky urban underground of New York. Madge is the unofficial matriarch of The Library, and when she raises her hand — like a rebel leader about to brief her loyal fighters on the blueprint of their next attack — she always gets called on. She has a dozen sponsees, a lightning-strike clarity, and an aura of cool that is as welcoming as it is daunting. Madge doesn't so much ever speak to me as she does grin, nod her head in my direction, and wink her non-patched eye to signal that she's watching and on my side. One generation older than Madge is Pam, who worked in fashion in the seventies and spent as much time at Studio 54 as Madge did at Max's. Though her era was the seventies and eighties, Pam has a gentle sixties-style vibe to her. Many of her sentences begin with *Oh, honey.* Her addictions were booze and pills, and what got her sober were her two kids, who were one or two benders away from being removed from her care by Social Services. Pam and Rafe and Madge are all sober for many years, but because of their schedules — Rafe is a nutritionist and singing coach, Madge is a counselor of some kind, and Pam does freelance fashion publicity — all come to the 12:30 and/or the two o'clock each day. I think of them as the Big Kids of the meeting and I'm both intimidated and comforted by them. I usually see Asa at the 12:30 and make sure we sit together. His class schedule allows him to go to meetings in the middle of the day, and sometimes he'll meet me here or at the Meeting House in the evening, after which we'll usually hang out at a coffeehouse on Greenwich Avenue or the diner on Seventh Avenue and 15th Street near my apartment.

When I look at Asa and Madge, it amazes me that such successful, happy, long-sober people still bother going to so many meetings. They seem as if they have it licked. I think back on my life when I was working and can't fathom how I'd have been able to fit as much recovery into my schedule as they do. Were there any sober people in book publishing? I can't remember any. That world seems forever closed to me now, but even if it wasn't, I think perhaps it's not a business one can stay sober in. I couldn't. When I came back from rehab in Oregon the year before, I went to one meeting a week, somehow couldn't manage that, and eventually went to none. I had a sponsor, but that guy wanted to meet every week and for me to call every day—just as Jack does now. I was busy and believed that the people who needed all these meetings and phone calls were either lonely or underemployed. I never shared or raised my hand in meetings then, never met one other person besides that sponsor whom my rehab arranged for me to meet when I returned to the city. When I tell Jack about trying to get sober a year ago, he says, *It sounds like ME versus THEM and never WE, and the only way to get and stay sober is when it becomes WE.* He also tells me that getting and staying sober—even after ninety days—needs to remain forever my first priority; that whatever I put in front of it I will eventually lose. *Career, family, boyfriend—all of it—you'll lose it. Lose again, in your case.* He tells me these things for the first time when he visits me in White Plains, and even though the words he is saying are as simple and basic as a child's box of crayons, I have no idea what he is talking about.

As I pace and fret in front of the Meeting House and watch crisp-suited, shiny-watched Chelsea residents scurry home from their day, it strikes me again, as it has more than once over the last few weeks, that I'm qualified to do absolutely nothing. I don't even have restaurant experience, save for the four days I waited tables in Connecticut after I was thrown out of school for spraying fire extinguishers in a drunken rampage with my housemates. I was fired on the fourth day of the job for lack of focus and dropping too many dishes. I think of all the pot I smoked back then—from morning until night—and I wonder how I was ever able to crawl out of that haze into any job, to go or get anywhere.

I have no retail experience, no bankable talents. I remember how a colleague at my first job in New York took copywriting courses at the Learning Annex, left publishing, and became a successful advertising executive. But this guy was brilliant, exceptionally brilliant, and that world would require, I imagine, schmoozing with potential clients, wooing new business over dinners and drinks, and without booze to get me through, it does not seem possible. Graduate school of any kind would be a decent way to delay the oncoming future, but with what money? How could I incur student loans on top of the already formidable and growing debt I've amassed from rehab, legal bills, and credit cards? Never mind that my third-tier college transcript is a speckled mess of mediocre grades and summer courses at the University of Connecticut to make up for the semester I lost when I was expelled. What graduate school would have me?

The custodian of the Meeting House has still not shown up to unlock the doors. I've left messages everywhere and still no one is picking up. The meeting begins in half an hour, and as my future prospects seem less and less appealing I start to think again of going to Mark's. It's the end of the day, Mark is no doubt ready to get high, and the dealers are about to turn their cell phones on. *Fuck it*, I say and start walking down 16th Street, away from the Meeting House, toward

Sixth Avenue, toward Mark's. I can feel the adrenaline spark through my veins and the doomy clouds of my futureless future begin to streak away. Just as I approach Sixth Avenue I see someone on the north side of 16th Street waving. It's Asa. Neat as a pin, fit as a fiddle, and heading right toward me. *You going to the meeting?* he chirps, and I can't muster an answer. He looks especially crisp today in his usual uniform. *What's going on?* he asks, and as I struggle to come up with something to say to get away from him, he puts his freckled hand on my upper arm and says, *OK, let's go.*

By the time we get to the Meeting House, the door has been unlocked and someone is inside making coffee. The dusty schoolhouse smell mingling with the aroma of cheap, freshly brewed coffee acts as an antidote to the giddy, pre-high adrenaline of just minutes before. The obsession to use fades just as quickly as it had arrived, and while I watch Asa help the old guy who's setting up the meeting move a bench to the far wall, it hits me how close I just came to relapsing, and what a miracle it is that he materialized precisely when he did. *Jesus, I'm sick,* I think. Unlike the people who can get sober on willpower, I need cheap coffee, church basements, serendipitous sidewalk interventions, and relapsing cokehead dog walkers. But what is most discouraging is that all these things and more — Jack, Polly, Madge, Asa, The Library, my family, my remaining friends, the staggering losses and humiliations of the past few months, the empire of people I've hurt—are still, it seems, not enough to keep me clean.

People come in from their day, mostly nine-to-five types who can't make the midday meetings like the ones at The Library. They start filling the chairs and benches of the large room which doubles, depending on the hour, as a Quaker meeting house, a dance studio, and a gathering space for other programs of recovery. Chic, chatty, confident—these people seem a world away from the struggles that must have brought them here. *How the hell did they do it?* I wonder, as I remember how close I just came to picking up. If Asa hadn't hauled me in from the street, I'd be right now pressing the buzzer at Mark's apartment. Right now waiting for him to buzz me in and hand me a crack pipe. It was Asa and nothing else that kept me from using just minutes ago.

I look around from sober face to sober face and wonder again how these people found their way. How will I? I sense that just being here and in places like it will not be enough. I'm in the room but not of it. Present but not a part of. Saved, for a little while, but not sober. Not really. I come like a beggar to these meetings and I'm fed, yes, pulled in off the street even, as I was today. But it's clear that something beyond my own need and ability to ask for help will keep me here, involve me in what is going on, connect me to something greater than my addiction, and give me a fighting chance of staying clean and getting on with my life. But what?

The meeting begins. As the basket is passed and people toss in their bills, I raise my hand and say that I have eight days, and as I do I know that eventually, not today, and probably not tonight, but at some point soon, I will pick up. I don't know what I'll do with my life, if I'll ever have a full-time job again, another love, where I'll live or even if I will, but I will use again, this much I know.

# The Mother Lode

My parents divorce the year I move to New York. I am twenty-one and they sell the deep-in-the-woods Connecticut house I grew up in and move to New Hampshire. They go there to save their marriage, but soon after they get settled, everything falls apart. It is my mother who leaves, finally, after years of threatening to, and in her flight back to Connecticut, as my father cancels credit cards and makes bank accounts inaccessible to her, she somehow lays her hands on a little pile of silver—ingots and coins they'd purchased as investments decades before.

A few years after their divorce is finalized, my mother gives me the silver to sell for her in the city. At the time, the market for precious metals is low and we decide to wait and sell later. The silver sits in the back of my closet for years in an old red and blue nylon knapsack I picked up in Scotland on my study-abroad semester in college. She asks about it occasionally but either I am too busy or it's not quite the right moment to sell. Eventually, she stops asking. The market crests and crashes dozens of times while the silver sits, unsold and unseen, in closets of apartments I move to in Midtown, the Upper East Side, Chelsea, and Greenwich Village. As I move, the silver moves. I forget it exists until I am packing up my things to leave One Fifth and see the familiar old knapsack. I don't remember, at first, what it holds but notice how unbelievably heavy it is when I pull it down from the shelf in the hall closet. It goes with the rest of my things to the studio on 15th Street, gets shoved to the back of another closet, and there it sits.

Meanwhile, my eight days become eleven and Polly's four become seven and then—after she joins Heather on a long, coke-crazed night—one. We raise our hands at The Library, count our days; people clap, encourage, and pass us their phone numbers. My routine calcifies: wake up, feed Benny, long workout at the gym, Library meetings at 12:30 and two o'clock, dog run with Polly, *Oprah*, Meeting House at six, diner dinner with Asa or others from the meeting, and phone calls to Jack, Kim, Asa, Jean, and Polly in between, before, and after. Once or twice a week I'll see Dave or Jean or Cy for dinner or a movie, but Jack has warned against straying too far outside the fold of recovery until I have ninety days. Bags of food arrive at least once a week from Jean, and when we see each other she'll ask if I enjoyed this or that and if there's anything special I'd like. I will never have much to say in response other than *Thank you*.

On Saturdays there is a 10:30 a.m. meeting that many people from The Library go to, and on Saturday evenings a big gay group that, God help me, because Asa goes, I go to. The skinny boys with white belts are crawling all over the Saturday night meeting. Rafe is usually there, too, always says *Bill* in his particular tone and clocks me in his laser-like way, making it clear he sees me far more clearly than I see myself. Most of these guys talk about dance clubs and Fire Island, and they're all young and cute and skinny, and I don't belong. I feel uncouth and lumpy and unkempt and listen only for the differences in their stories, not the similarities. I'm gay but in this place I feel as if there's a manual for gays that covers everything from clothes, hairstyle, and slang to eating, drinking, and using habits, and everyone in the room owns it but me. I tell Jack this one night on the phone and he asks me if there have been other experiences, other times, when I felt as if I never got the manual. When I think back to high school, college, book publishing, crack dens even— every world I entered—I felt exactly the same way: that there was a set of rules, a primer of some kind, that everyone else had read and understood but I had never seen. Like so many of my worries, Jack tells me, this one—right down to the word *manual*—is one of the bedrock feelings of most alcoholics and addicts. Again I'm relieved in some way, but also humiliated and annoyed that most everything I complain about he is able to label and place within both his own experience and the broader population of alcoholics and addicts. *You're just a garden variety junkie,* he tells me yet again and says good night.

At one of the gay meetings I meet, or re-meet, a guy named Luke whom I met a few times through mutual friends over the years and who, to my surprise, is sober. He's a screenwriter, my age, has a sober boyfriend, and has stories of using that make me wish we'd gotten sloppy together at least a few times. He feels like family from the second we reconnect, and even though he is only a year and a half sober, he seems like one of the Big Kids, like Madge and Rafe and Pam. Luke went to college with Noah and they know each other vaguely. The mutual friends, Noah connection, and similar stories of using make Luke one of the few people from the rooms who bridge both my old life and new. Everyone else is a world away from book publishing and my life with Noah, which is mainly a relief, but sometimes, when I am trying to relate details of the life I lived and ruined to people like Polly and Asa, it can be frustrating. When I try to explain this frustration to Jack, he just laughs and says, *Honey, keep coming back* (an expression, minus the *honey,* people use in the rooms, usually when people counting days raise their hands and share).

So. The silver. It just sits there. I bump into it a few times while pulling shoes down from the upper shelf of the closet, or knock against it as I'm putting away some blanket or box. This is Mom's, I remind myself each time, not mine. I have a few thousand dollars in my account—money remaining from a former client who repaid money I'd loaned her last year to cover an unexpected tax bill. Kim contacts the former client when I'm in Lenox Hill and miraculously a big chunk of cash materializes just as a deposit is needed for rehab. It is only in the last week that Kim has transferred the remaining money—just a little over two thousand dollars—into my checking account.

After the deposit at the rehab (which represents less than a quarter of the total bill, which they've agreed to let me pay back over time), the next big expense is the apartment. The deposit on the apartment and the broker's fee came from money I borrowed from Elliot—a guy I had an affair with a few years before, who became a friend. He lived with his ex-boyfriend a few blocks from One Fifth and they had, a few years back, broken up. The affair is short and boozy and ends weeks after it began on a weekend when Noah is away. Afterward, we become friends and see each other for dinner every few months or so. I don't see Elliot much in the six months preceding my relapse, but once I make it to White Plains he is one of the few people other than Jean who visit on a regular basis. He comes on the weekends to play tennis on the cracked, weed-choked asphalt slabs that pass for courts. We play for a while and walk the grounds. We don't talk much, but the distraction of the game and the easy air between us are welcome reprieves from the tormenting thoughts of my recent history and my all-too-near future. Elliot arrives each time with tennis racquets in hand and little gesture toward or judgment of the dark path that led me here. Elliot is exactly my age, exactly my height, similarly featured and colored, but has an enviable midwestern openness and ease that I don't possess. Elliot runs a highly respected nonprofit organization, we have virtually no one in common, and besides Dave and Jean and Julia and Cy, he is one of my few remaining friends. My once crowded life has dwindled to a few resilient stragglers. Elliot is one.

So Elliot lends me the money for the first month's rent, deposit, and broker's fee. I ask him because before I return to New York, he offers to lend me money if I need it. Some last scrap of vanity has kept me from going into my financial problems with him but he clearly detects trouble. At the time that he offers, asking Elliot for money seems out of the question, but weeks later he'll be the one person I think I can ask. I can't ask Dave for one more favor or helping hand, as he's at the breaking point already, and I can't risk losing Jean's friendship—especially not now when I have so few people left. I have a strong sense that if I asked her, it'd be curtains. Her wealth, I imagine, must be a familiar elephant in the room, a known animal brushing against most interactions. Now that I'm wiped out financially, it suddenly becomes, between us, an entire herd.

The first day Jean visits me in White Plains we go for a walk. As we walk I complain about how I'm not sure I can return to New York because I have no money, not sure I can stay in the rehab because it's so expensive, not sure I won't have to move in with my sister in Maine, and not sure

I'll ever crawl out from under the mountain of debt that has risen since the day I relapsed two months ago. It's all I talk about because at the moment it's all I can think about. As we're walking Jean stiffens and goes quiet. She swats an invisible fly from her face and she doesn't turn to look at me when I ask her if she's OK. The elephant has its hoof on her throat and suddenly I recognize that the only way to make it go away is to name it. Loudly. So I blurt out something about how I'm suddenly poor, getting poorer by the second, and that I'm terrified. That I'm going to need to talk about being terrified with my friends, and since she's one of the few I have left, I need to be able to worry to her without her thinking I'm doing so because I want her to solve the problem. *So ditch me because I'm tedious, but not because you're worried I want you to bail me out.* I don't remember what she says to this but I remember her laughing, and that by the time we returned from our walk, the elephants had lumbered away.

So I return to New York, see the studio on 15th Street, and even though the rent is pretty cheap, I can't afford it. The landlord and broker need all that money. Since Jean and Dave are out, and because most of my family is broke, I ask Elliot. The first time in my adult life I've asked anyone for money, and Elliot's *yes* is as uncomplicated as if I'd asked him for a French fry off his dinner plate. As uncomfortable as the asking is, as grim as the circumstances are that bring me to the question, the yes is a miracle. The yes, with all its confidence and kindness, is like Jane's kiss on the street near One Fifth, or Jean's bags of food. It cuts through the plaque of shame and reminds me that somewhere underneath the wretched addict is a person worth being kind to, even worth betting on. And I do not look like a good bet, that much is clear from any perspective, but when I tell Elliot I don't know when I'll be able to pay him back, he just says, *I'm not worried. I know you will.*

With Elliot's money, May's rent is paid. I have no idea where June will come from. I'm eleven days sober, have a couple of grand in the bank, and with less than two weeks before it's time to pay next month's rent, I remember the silver. Of course, *the silver.* I'll sell the silver, pay the rent for June and July at least, and pay my mother back someday, somehow. At coffee after the Meeting House that night I ask Luke if he knows of a place that buys silver and he tells me about a guy on 25th Street between Sixth Avenue and Broadway. As soon as he says the address my stomach tightens: it's in one of Jack's off-limits trigger zones, just a few doors down from the office building where our literary agency had been. I don't say anything to Luke, but as I head toward home that night I think, I won't tell Jack and I'll just get it over with.

The next day, I grab my little blue and red knapsack and head up Sixth. The store is a combination pawnshop and rug showroom. It's huge and dark with great piles of carpets rising from the dusty floors and spider plants withering in the window. As I wait for someone to come out from behind the piles of rugs to help me, I imagine how many unseen rooms like this exist in the city, spaces behind doors I'll walk by a thousand times and never see. Since coming back, I've been amazed by how little I'd noticed before. Streets I'd walked on for ten years and never saw what was on them: pink town houses, eighteenth-century synagogues, ceramic shops, spectacular doorknobs, Italian bookshops. As with so much, I had been aware of so little off my narrow path or outside my own limited world. And there are so many worlds—fashion, academia, real estate, dance, education, firefighting, finance, advertising—each feeling, I imagine, like the center of the universe. All these separate and self-contained worlds making up entire cities within the city, coursing alongside and invisible to one another. *How is this occurring to me for the first time?* I wonder. How small my life and the world it happened within both seem now. What I know: book publishing, restaurants that serve vodka, crack dealers and crack dens. Bookstores, literary agencies, rug-strewn, book-crammed living rooms of editors and authors; gloomy apartments where people smoke themselves into shaky shadows, these I know. And now there are all the meeting rooms where I go each day and the diners and coffee shops we descend on in packs after. But these are just the tip of the iceberg. There are the rooms for sex addicts and crystal meth addicts and debtors, and the rooms for all the people who love them—a whole empire of rooms filling regularly, every hour of every day and with no one paying or getting paid to be there. Invisible cities, invisible rooms we pass by until by way of desperation or desire or ultimatum they are revealed to us. Like this room—a dusty cavern with spider plants, Persian rugs, and now a knapsack filled with silver.

A middle-aged man with a trim beard, dark skin, and a bright, singsong voice comes out and says hello and can he help me. I unpack the silver and after he's inspected each ingot and coin he pulls out a calculator and begins to elegantly tap the keys until, after a minute or two, he turns the face of the gadget to me and on its screen is a figure just north of six thousand dollars. Nearly three months' rent, I calculate, and right away, without pausing, I say, *Deal*.

After he slowly writes out a detailed receipt and cuts me a check, I rush to the nearest Chase branch—the one at Sixth Avenue and 23rd Street—and deposit it into my checking account. I go to the teller instead of an ATM, thinking the money will make its way into my account faster. I hand over the check, grab my second receipt of the day, and head toward the door. I enter the small vestibule that separates the inside of the bank from the street. I've been here before, hundreds of times—it's the branch where Kate and I opened the business and client trust accounts for the agency—but suddenly I remember the last time I visited, over two months before, deep in the bender that landed me in the emergency room at Lenox Hill. I remember that I'd run out of drugs and exceeded my ATM limit for the day, so with passport and cash card in hand, I rushed to this branch. Rough from many sleepless nights and crashing from more than an hour without a hit, I withdrew three thousand dollars, stuffed it in the upper front pocket of my black Arcteryx jacket, and headed for the door. In my hurry I failed to notice that the zipper on the bottom of the pocket was unzipped, and when I stepped out of the bank into the vestibule, the cash dropped from my jacket. With air rushing through the doors on either side of me, the money flew everywhere. Hundred-dollar bills, mostly. I remember how, for a moment, it didn't look real and I was mesmerized. It looked like one of those game show challenges where people are put in a chamber of wind-tossed cash and they have thirty seconds to grab as much as they can. But when I saw a hundred-dollar bill fly out the door into the street I snapped to life.

Standing here, two months later, I picture my thin, wrecked, desperate self, scrambling to collect a windstorm of bills. I remember sweat pouring down my face, and the blasts of cold air coming in from the street. I remember a guy with a bike helmet on and two young women helping me collect the money. I remember putting the wad of bills back into the same pocket and its falling out again, but this time the guy with the bike helmet pounces and prevents the bills from flying. *You OK?* he asks doubtfully, and as I double-check the zippers I see my hands—stained black from scraping charred wire screens, blistered with lighter burns, and scabbed all over from nicks and cuts from dozens of shattered glass stems. I shove the money in my jacket pocket again, hide my hands in my jeans, and, not knowing how to respond, hurry to the street.

I try to remember where in the vestibule I was that day and how long it took to collect the bills. People—now in late spring clothes, not bundled for winter as they were then— pass in and out of the bank in front of me, and I try to picture one of them dropping three thousand dollars' worth of cash. Twice. I try to imagine what I would do and how I'd react. How on earth did I not get arrested? It seems so cartoonish and unlikely, so far away.

Further away is the memory of me and Kate meeting in this same space before sitting down with a bank officer to open the accounts we needed to start the agency. How many years ago was this? Four? Five? Three? I can't remember, and I can't see us then. It's too painful or too long ago, but in either case I can catch only the edges of that day, the conspiratorial air, the excitement and trust that passed between us. The hope.

I leave the little time machine bank vestibule and step out into the warm afternoon. It's almost three and I have three hours to kill before the six o'clock meeting at the Meeting House. I'm hungry and exhausted and think, fuck it, the Meeting House can survive with one less junkie tonight. I think this even though I'd agreed to meet Polly there. *I'm not a babysitter,* I say out loud, feeling the giddy rush of deciding to skip the meeting pushing away the heavy memories of just a few moments ago. *I'm no one's keeper!* I go on, declaring to the air like a lunatic.

As I walk home, I wonder how long it will take the check to clear, how long before the six thousand dollars will add to the two thousand in the account already and make eight. Eight thousand seems like an enormous amount of money. More than three months' rent. The apartment would be covered into the fall, and with bags of food from Jean, I'll be OK past October. The bank is at 23rd Street and Sixth Avenue. My apartment is at 15th Street and Seventh Avenue. Somewhere south of 20th and north of 16th I remember again that day two months ago, leaving the bank with three thousand dollars stuffed in my jacket, calling Rico from the street and telling him to meet me at my room at the Gansevoort Hotel. I remember him saying he was only a block away and how my heart raced as I hailed a cab to get there before he did, how his van was pulling up to the hotel just as my cab was, and how I hopped from one vehicle right into the other. From call to cab to van and back to my room took less than five minutes, some kind of record, and in the middle of the day, no less. Remembering the return to the hotel room, the wealth of drugs, the remaining cash in hand, and the night ahead starts my heart racing. I think again of the two thousand in my account. The two that will be eight. Following the thousand-dollar-a-day logic of those nights at the Gansevoort, three months' rent becomes eight nights high. Eights nights less the thousand I owe Rico and the thousand I owe Happy. Six nights high. If I call one of them now and pay back what I owe I'll still have a grand in cash to buy drugs. And I won't have to go to Mark's like last time and suffer through his jittery lectures and treacherous friends.

I arrive at my building, enter the lobby, and hit the elevator button. Somewhere between the lobby and the seventeenth floor, three months' rent becomes seven digits. Seven forgotten digits that bubble up from memory like a dark miracle that I dial on my new phone which, until now, has not stored or dialed any dealer's phone numbers. After a few rings, Happy picks up with a question, *Who is this?* I tell him.

_____

Happy takes his time getting to the apartment. On the phone I let him know right away I have the money I owe him and that I need to buy a thousand dollars' worth of drugs. I give him the new address and he hangs up the phone. It's three in the afternoon and he shows up after eleven. I call him a few times through the afternoon and evening, but he doesn't pick up. I pace the studio and avoid phone calls from Polly and Jack while I wait with the two thousand dollars I ran back to the bank to get. Though eight hours pass from the initial phone call to hearing him knock on the apartment door, there is no turning back from getting high. It's like a switch has been flipped and I'm on autopilot. No phone call, second thought, or imagined consequence can keep me from doing what I'm about to do. Only Happy not showing up can keep me from using, and if he doesn't show up by midnight, I've already decided that I'll go to Mark's.

At eleven there's a knock at the door. There he is, looking exactly as he always has: white sweatpants, black hooded sweatshirt, Yankees cap, and large headphones around his neck. Without saying a word, he walks past me into the apartment and looks around. *Smaller place,* he says, in a voice that is both empty of and bursting with opinion. *Wondered where you went,* he adds with a hard emphasis on *went,* as I hand him the cash he doesn't count. He pulls out ten bags and two stems from the front pocket of his sweatpants and as he hands them to me says, *It's good,* and starts for the door. Usually two hundred bucks gets you two bags plus a third bag free, so I say, cautiously, *Aren't there five missing? Interest,* he answers, simply and without turning around, before he palms the door and steps into the hall. I watch him go and wait to hear the elevator open and shut before I go to the door and double-lock it.

From the first hit, which I load with as much as I once would have used in a whole night, there is something wrong. Something off. The drug tastes like medicine, and while, yes, there is a wallop of something blasting through my lungs and heart and brain, it's not the high I've waited for since three o'clock. After exhaling a huge plume of smoke, I light up and inhale another deep lungful. And then another. I pull so hard and inhale so deeply that on the fifth hit the stem pops apart from the excessive heat. I'm high but exactly where I started, still here and not there. And *there* is the only place I want to be, a place where no amount of this smoke can take me. Is it the drug or is it me? I can't tell what's wrong but something is. I call Happy and tell him that there's something not right with what he sold me and ask him if he'll switch the bags. I lie and tell him I'm about to start a period when I'll be ordering a lot more and this is not a great place to start. By one in the morning Happy shows up again. He's smiling, as if I've passed some test, and not angry as I thought he'd be. I've smoked down one bag and give him the remaining nine. He hands me back ten new ones that I can tell are colored and textured differently. He doesn't say one word from the moment he enters the apartment to the moment he leaves. I say *Thank you* as he goes and then lock the door, take a clean stem, and pack it to the brim. I can instantly tell the difference when I inhale the new smoke and the freight train I've been waiting for all day finally hits me. At last, the world cracks open and I fall through, leaving behind for a blessed second everything and everyone. I settle into the couch and, with eyes closed, hold on to what I know will be over soon. It will wriggle away as suddenly as it arrives, just as it always does, and I will, I know, sit on this couch for hours, burning my fingers and filling my lungs to court its return. But it never does. What comes instead is restlessness followed by an urgent need to get out of the apartment. What comes after that are two Asian guys—young, hip, bored, cute—standing in front of a white tile apartment building down the block from mine, who seem to be waiting for me. I ask them to come over and they do. I ask them if they get high and they say yes. I show them a stem and they ask what it is. I suggest they try, and they do. They both get naked and I join them and the hours pass as the three of us thrash around on the bed and stop and start dozens of times to get high and down vodka. At around ten in the morning I am convinced they are undercover cops or DEA agents who have tricked me into letting them into my apartment, and I demand that they leave. They are confused, ask for a stem and a bag of drugs, which I refuse, and at last they go. I sneak to the liquor store on Seventh Avenue and buy two half gallons of vodka and a bag of ice. I drink the first bottle quickly and close my eyes and fall asleep for a couple of hours. I have five bags left and I stuff a quarter of the contents of one into a pipe and begin to hope, like so many times before, that my heart explodes, that my brain erupts, and that the death dance can resolve, for once and finally, in death. I look across my small studio to the door that leads to the terrace and remember the first thought I had when I saw it, weeks ago, when the real estate agent showed me the apartment: if all else fails, there's that.

Wednesday becomes Thursday. Five bags become three. The lighter, bent down at an angle too far and for too long, pops, and its metal workings explode apart in my hand. It is the last lighter and it's now evening again. I scan a few drawers and pockets and find no more and realize I have to go out. I pour a vodka and look around at the apartment filled with glasses jammed with cigarette butts the Asian guys must have smoked. There are used condoms on the floor, a sheet nailed to the wall above the terrace door to block anyone seeing in, and empty beer cans and vodka bottles everywhere. The gloom of the wrecked room and the grim image of three strangers drugging and drinking and slamming into each other to create closeness or apartness or whatever each of us is running to or toward is too much to bear. And there is nothing new about it. It's like every other time getting high. And here I am again. I look at the terrace door. I look at the bags of drugs on the coffee table and think: Is there enough to get me on the other side? Is there enough to finish what I started two months ago? There's only one way to find out, I decide, as I put on my shoes to go get lighters.

Like every other time I've left a room with drugs, I worry it will be raided, and more than the fear of being arrested, I panic at the idea that the drugs will be seized, taken away, not used. So I tuck the bags in the front pocket of my shorts, put on a clean T-shirt, wash my hands to clear off the soot, and leave. The elevator man, the older of the two Serbian brothers who work the elevator in the building, mumbles something inaudible. I pray he can't smell the smoke I've been breathing for nearly forty-eight hours. I leave the building and immediately wish I hadn't. The sidewalks along Seventh Avenue are teeming with people. Cars streak by, sirens sound, voices come from all directions. I don't want to be here, but I need lighters and have no choice. I get to the bodega and ask for ten lighters, more than I need but I'm fearful I'll run out again. Once I have them in my pockets I walk back to Seventh Avenue, head south, and before I've turned onto 15th Street, I see him. Asa.

How he persuades me to come to his apartment I have no idea. I'm standing in his small studio living room listening to him talk to his sponsor, Lucy. I hear him say the word *Be-*

*nadryl* and I can't imagine why. I go to the bathroom and run the water and flush the toilet while I draw as big a hit as I can. Immediately he comes knocking on the door. I pack another hit, light it, and exhale as I scramble unsuccessfully to find a window to open. The little room is dense with smoke, and when I open the door the drug clouds pour into the apartment like steam. Asa is calm and not confrontational but he asks me, gently, if I will give him the drugs. I say I should probably leave, but as I do I think I hear heavy footfalls outside his door. One part of me is aware that I am becoming paranoid, as I always do on drugs, and the other remembers the Asian guys who seemed to be communicating with each other last night in an intricate code of winks and hand signals. And then the shadows on the terrace that looked like men with bulletproof vests.

Asa has a box of Benadryl in his hand and says that Lucy suggests I take a few to kill the edge, soften the high, and help bring me down a little so I can decide what to do. This sounds good, so I ask for three and I swallow them down. I ask if he has alcohol in the house, and as I do I remember how we know each other—from the rooms—and I apologize. But I know that I need alcohol and I need it soon. *I need to go to the bathroom*, I say, and he seems genuinely stumped, so he turns his back and starts talking again to Lucy. I disappear into the bathroom and load up the stem a few more times. I feel a notch calmer as the hits push away some of the worry, but in its place comes something else. That old restless sexual energy that this drug unleashes. So I go back out to where Asa is and say I'm getting warm. I ask him if it's OK if I take my T-shirt off and he just sort of blinks and says, *I guess so.* I'm feeling a bit bolder now than before, so after my shirt is off I pull out a stem and pack it in front of him and draw a hit. I exhale into the neat, attractive little studio. I pull a chair directly in front of where he's sitting on the couch and lean back and put my hands in my pockets. I push my shorts down my hips a little and flex my arms and think that something is about to happen. In the deluding inner sheen of the high, I think there's no way he won't be game to fool around. I've had a sense he may have a crush on me and by God if he does, here I am. It seems completely logical, and Asa the friend, the saving angel, the sober comrade disappears and in his place is just a beautiful nearby body that looks like the next place to go in my crack-mapped journey. He hands me another Benadryl and asks me again if he can take the drugs from me. Again, he's calm, not angry or pushy. But I can barely hear him for all my desire. He stays on the phone with Lucy and says to me, *You can stop now. You can stop and you can crash here and everything will be OK. This doesn't have to get any worse than it already is.*

Something in his tone strikes a nerve. *What if this could be over?* I think, and then remember the terrace off my apartment, the seventeen floors down to the asphalt of 15th Street. A few hours ago, that was the only way I could see to end this. Now here's Asa offering another way. But that way—the meetings and the diners and the phone calls and the sponsor and the off-limits trigger zones all over the city—that way is not working. Here I am with my shirt off, two and a half bags away from smoking a thousand dollars' worth of crack, hitting on and trying to relapse someone who has only extended to me kindness and patience and time. I am doing everything I can to seduce him into the very oblivion that nearly destroyed him years ago. Asa asks me where I got the money for the drugs and I tell him about the pile of silver but I don't tell him it was my mother's. Some alchemy of Benadryl, the mention of the silver, and Asa's patient tones spook the sexual weather away.

Confused and desperate for another hit, I tell Asa I need to take a shower. He gets me a towel, asks me not to smoke the drugs in the bathroom, which I agree to, and then, once the water is running, pack a fresh hit and try to force enough smoke into my system so I can figure out what to do. The water pipes creak as I turn up the hot water and through that noise I soon hear another noise—voices, men's voices, coming from the other side of the wall. Are they in the hallway? The next apartment? The dread of being under surveillance that has come in and out like a tide over the last forty-eight hours shows up again, suddenly and full force. There are voices coming from behind two walls now. I hear *Let's get him* and *Why are we waiting?* and I turn off the water to listen closely. Asa's at the door and says, *OK, that's enough, come on out.* And then I think: *He's in on it. These guys, whoever they are, are with him.* I scramble into my clothes, flush the toilet, and take another hit with what's left of the third bag. Thinking there may be drug agents and police on the other side of the door, I hide the last two bags, lighter, and stem in the medicine cabinet. *I'll say it's Asa's,* I think diabolically, pulling the cabinet door shut and confronting in the mirror what would be obvious to anyone: a desperate addict. Asa knocks, and his careful voice comes from the other side.

In a cramped, smoke-filled studio bathroom in Chelsea, one of three things is about to happen: arrest, returning home to a seventeen-story exit from everything, or giving the drugs to Asa and trusting that what he's saying is true. That I'll be OK. That this is just a stumble and not a fall. I look in the mirror again and see what I always see when I'm high: my eyes, dead and black and staring back as if they were someone or something else's eyes and not my own. I sway before the mirror and begin to feel the Benadryl crawl underneath the drugs and link hands with the sleepless hours of the nights before. I step to the door and open it. On the other side it's Asa, alone, no one else, no men in bulletproof vests wielding guns and handcuffs. I decide to give up. I know if I do, there will be no more voices on the other side of the wall. At least for now.

My eleven days become one and Polly's one becomes four. The eight grand becomes six and the messages on my phone are too many to count. June's rent is due in two weeks. After June is paid there will be $3,500 left in the account with four weeks until July's rent is due. How did I go from having nearly four months' rent covered to barely two? I know, I just don't want to remember. But as much as I try, the last three days keep flickering to life. The Asian guys I picked up off the street, got high with, and threw out. Which night was that? Tuesday? Wednesday? It's not clear. The voices behind the bathroom wall at Asa's. Asa. Taking my shirt off and trying to seduce him. And then the final deal he and I strike: that I'll give him the drugs if he allows me to smoke one more hit, which I do, in a chair, in front of him, while he sits on the couch and watches, cell phone and sponsor pressed to his ear. I give him the remaining bags and watch him flush them down the toilet. Watch him smash the stem and flush the glass. Afterward, Asa walks me home and spends the rest of the night on my couch. We wake up late the next morning, and after I feed Benny, he walks me to the corner of Fifth and 10th Street so I can go to the 12:30 meeting at The Library. He rushes to class, and I promise I'll see him at the two o'clock meeting.

I can't bear the idea of walking into The Library and counting one day, so I circle the block a few times. My mother keeps calling, and I wonder if she knows that I've relapsed again. I have not yet listened to any of the messages. I call Jack and tell him what's happened. He sounds tired when he tells me to go to meetings all day and raise my hand. The rest can wait. Eventually, but not now, I will call Kim and Dave and Jean and Polly and Luke and everyone else who I suspect has left messages and who will have to decide whether to stick with me or step away.

I go to the meeting, but since I wait until the last possible moment to enter the building, by the time I get to the fifth floor the place is packed and it takes a long, uncomfortable minute to find a seat. Looking through the crowded room I don't see anyone I know. I then see Pam, who motions toward the far back wall where there is an empty seat. It's next to Annie, someone I met just a few days before. She's the one I saw that first day at The Library and was convinced I'd met somewhere before. At first I thought she was the girlfriend of Noah's screenwriting partner, but a week later, when I gathered enough courage to say hello, it turned out we'd never met. She has a little more time than I have and is, like me, not working and doing nothing else but getting sober. She's recently completed a two-year MFA program in acting, but she went on a bender two nights before her showcase performance, where the school invites agents and managers. Her acting partner had to go on with one of the professors reading from a script, and because the showcase is one of the requirements for getting a degree, she has not yet officially graduated. There was a messy period that followed the showcase disaster before she found her way into the rooms.

———

*Hey, lambchop,* she whispers as I sit down. Annie is wearing, as usual, a thrift store ensemble of Rickie Lee Jones–style beret, a big-plastic-buttoned purple cardigan sweater, and denim overalls. *Long time no talk,* she says.

The meeting starts. At the break, I raise my hand and announce that I have one day and Pam gasps above the clapping, *Oh, honey.* In between the 12:30 and the two o'clock, I finally listen to my messages. It's a familiar series of regular check-in messages that, one by one, lose their carefree tone and crumble from concern to anger. My mother leaves three or four and the last one is a doozy. She is crying and she is angry and she shouts more than says, *You have stolen from me and you need to call me right away.* I haven't seen my mother since an afternoon last year when she left me in a restaurant after I brought up some difficult and never before spoken-about memories from my childhood. Since then we've barely talked and I have not seen her. I ask her, through my sister Kim, not to come to Lenox Hill while I am there, and when she offers to visit me in rehab and in the city after I return, again I tell her, through Kim, that I'd rather she did not.

Before the day in the restaurant I'd always been her faithful lieutenant in the ongoing war with my father. Never questioned her side of things, stood by her in the divorce, and generally agreed with her version of events, whatever they were. But with the marvels of therapy, a pushy counselor in rehab, and the miracle of suppressed memory, all that changed in the last year. Her tone with me—in voice mail messages, mostly—since that lunch has been conciliatory, careful, wounded. I cannot remember her ever being angry with me. We had always been on each other's side. Me, Kim, and Mom against Dad. It was fun when he was away on a trip, tense when he returned. He was the dark one, she the light. When I was thrown out of college he was the one who delivered the harsh lecture and she the one who comforted me afterward. When I skipped school she rolled her eyes and wagged a finger, but she was never hard or harsh or punishing. So this message she leaves, short though it is, packs a hard, jarring punch.

I'm standing on the corner of 10th Street and University, not sure whether to return her call or go to the two o'clock meeting. How on earth does she know about the silver? I run through all the possibilities and come up with nothing. Are there serial numbers on silver ingots and coins? Did some precious metals office call her to confirm the sale? Thinking about government agencies triggers the paranoia from the night before, and in addition to feeling hungover, defeated, and ashamed, I start to feel that old nagging dread of being observed. I turn to walk home, and before I get more than a few steps down 10th, I hear Annie call my name. She stands on the corner looking like a pint-sized host of some public access kids' TV show—red lipstick, goofy beret, lace-up

Converse high-tops, jumbo overalls, megawatt smile. *Get over here, lamb, you're not going anywhere.*

Annie and I go to Newsbar, a small coffee and Internet café just a few blocks up University from The Library. She asks me why I look so spooked, and as I start to tell her about my mother, the silver, the rug guy from 25th Street, and the six thousand dollars, I notice two middle-aged guys in windbreakers sitting three tables away, listening to what I'm saying. Just then a woman with what looks like an earpiece enters the place, and I grab Annie's hand and tell her we have to go. *Now.* She doesn't blink or react, just says, *Gotcha, I'll follow you.* We rush to the street, and as we head toward Union Square, I notice Annie is still holding my hand. *I'm not crazy,* I tell her and she pats my arm. *Of course you're not, lamby,* she whispers, as if letting me in on a secret. *You're insane.*

When we get to Union Square I stop us in the middle of the steps on the south side and check and recheck to make sure there is no one within earshot. Still holding my hand Annie says, *OK, we're safe, now tell me what's going on.* So I tell her. Everything. My parents' difficult marriage, the buried memories from childhood, my mother leaving me in a restaurant

last year, the time at Newark airport and after when I believed I was being followed by DEA agents, trying to kill
myself after two months in hotel rooms smoking crack, the
silver, calling Happy, the terrace off my studio and the returning thoughts of suicide, the voices at Asa's, and finally
my mother's phone message. Annie takes it all in and then
says, laughing a little and still, and tightly now, holding my
hand, *That's one mother of a mother lode.* She pulls me down
onto the steps to sit down. *I'm not going to even pretend I understood half of what you just said, but what you need to do right
now is call your mother and listen to whatever she's got to say
and then be honest and apologize. It's no more complicated than
that. So let's go. Where's your phone?* If Annie said I needed
to set my shoes on fire and sing Christmas carols I probably
would. She has been sober only a little while longer than I
have and has, from what I've heard of her share at The Library, seemed just as lost, but now, here, she seems like a
Great Elder of sobriety.


I call my mother. She can barely talk she's so upset. She
tells me that Asa called my sister, whose number I gave him
weeks ago in case of emergency. He called to tell her I had
relapsed but that I was OK. When my sister asked where
I got the money from, he said he knew I had recently sold
some silver. When my sister, who didn't know about the sil-

ver and assumed it was mine, tells my mother, she explodes. And now, she explodes all over again. *How could you do it?* she demands, sounding, within her rage, genuinely bewildered. *I don't know,* is all I have as a response, and *I'm sorry.*

As I'm getting off the call she says in the sternest voice I've ever heard her speak in, *Enough is enough, you've got to stop this. Stop it right now. Do you hear me? Enough is enough.* As much as I had dreaded the phone call, this last instruction, this line drawn, by my mother of all people— this girl-woman my sister and I took care of as kids, whom I've defended my whole life and avoided most of my adulthood—feels like something I've been missing for a long time but hadn't realized until now. Like how you don't know how hungry you've been until you see food, or how tired you are until your head hits a pillow.

Annie walks me back to The Library and hugs me goodbye. I agree to call her before going to sleep and rush into the building to catch the last half hour of the two o'clock meeting. I manage to get a seat next to Polly, who makes well-look-who-showed-up eyes at me. Asa is there, looking tired from being awake most of the night before. After the meeting he tells me matter-of-factly that he's spending the

night again at my place and that he'll pick me up there to go
to the Meeting House at six. All I can manage is *Thank you.*

Polly slaps me in the head and says, *What the fuck, Crackhead?* We walk to the dog run and I tell her what happened.
She listens and nods and is in no way surprised. *Just keep
coming back and next time, call me, OK? I promise you won't
want to use once I'm through with you.* She comes over to my
place for a while until Asa shows up. Asa and I go to the
Meeting House and come back to my place afterward and
eat quiche and roast chicken from the bags of food from
Jean that arrived while we were out. While Asa unfolds
the pullout bed from the couch, I call Jack to give an ac-
counting of the day—the meetings, talking to Polly and
Annie and Asa, apologizing to my mother, counting one
day at The Library—to which he responds, *Do it all again
tomorrow.* After I say good night and hang up the phone,
Asa turns off the lights and we crawl under our respec-
tive covers. Benny curls against the door, as far from me as
possible.

I can't sleep. Can't help but run through the events of the
last three days. Everything that followed the phone call to
Happy—the bad high, the good high, the Asian guys, the

broken stems, the vodka, the ruined lighters, the paranoia, the thoughts of suicide—is familiar, follows the same desperate script of every time using. But what's different, what is completely new, is what happens after. I realize that from the moment I ran into Asa on the street twenty-four hours ago, I have not been alone. After Asa I'm with Annie and after Annie with Polly and now, again, with Asa, who is asleep on my pullout couch.

I lie in bed, awake, in the dark. I can make out the edges of the white sheet that I'd nailed to the wall above the terrace door to cover its small window. One of the corners has come off and I watch it flap against the door, making shapes and movements that remind me of the cops and DEA agents I was convinced were lining up on the terrace two nights ago. I curl against the window next to the bed and try to blink away the thoughts of what would have happened without Asa. I remember him sitting across from me at the New Venus diner on my first night back in the city, how I had no intention of going with those boys to dinner, how Jack made me, and how it was Asa who told me to meet him the next day at The Library, which was where I met Polly and Annie. How are these people, whom I didn't know less than a month ago, how are they now the most important people in my life? My mind races with how unlikely it all seems, how arbitrary.

The room and the city outside are quiet. I listen to the sound of Asa's rough breathing and look out the window to the Empire State Building. The old skyscraper goes dark at midnight, as usual, but as it does this time the remaining lights in the skyline appear to blink awake, shine with new energy, as if each one has agreed now to shoulder the heavy burden of lighting the city, pick up the slack as one of their own tires out, realizes that he cannot, could never, do it on his own.

# Use

Polly has eight days and I have five. Though neither of us can put together longer than two weeks, we talk about what we'll do when we reach ninety. Polly may go back to teaching or working with animals. I have no idea what I'll do— little seems possible, and as my bank account thins and my debt thickens, the only solution seems to be to go live with my sister Kim in Maine. What I'll do there I can't imagine. How long she and her family would tolerate me is also unclear. Polly has a different predicament. Her sister Heather somehow lucked into their rent-controlled apartment on St. Mark's Place when she was in graduate school and the rent, by New York standards, is practically free. So there's less pressure on Polly to make money, but if Heather doesn't get sober it's not a place Polly's sponsor or anyone else at The Library recommends she remain. Her attachment to Heather is powerful—they are twins *and* using buddies—and up until recently, anytime I or anyone else suggests she move out Polly goes cold and swiftly changes the subject. But Heather continues to do lines of coke and stay up all night watching DVDs of *Law & Order*. Polly puts a few days together and, this time, becomes more open to talking about moving. By mid-May she begins mentioning—tentatively, cautiously—that she might look on Craigslist for apartments in Queens, which she's heard are cheap.

And then Polly disappears. She doesn't show up at either the 12:30 meeting or the two o'clock. I call and leave messages on her cell phone but get no answer. This goes on for days until her voice mail is full and stops accepting messages. I walk down St. Mark's and linger in front of her building, hoping to see her or Heather. Jack tells me not to buzz the apartment because I'm not even a week sober and there could be coke all over Polly's place. As much as I agree with his logic, there is no part of me that finds getting high with Polly appealing. There is no part of the prospect of coke in her apartment that triggers a craving. But I follow Jack's rules, even though I'm terrified she has overdosed. I call her sponsor, who says she hasn't heard from Polly but that someone from The Library saw Heather on the street, who said she's OK and to let her be.

So I do. The meetings at The Library for the rest of the week seem strange without Polly. The afternoons are more spacious. I go to coffee with Annie after the two o'clock meeting a few times, but it's odd not to go to the dog run, odd to be home for the beginning of the *Oprah* show at four o'clock each day. The weekend rolls around and Saturday morning, on a whim, I call Polly. Miraculously, she answers. *Hey, Crackhead,* she says, without the usual pluck, and I say, lamely, *If that's not the pot calling the crackhead black then I don't know what is.* She laughs but her voice is rough and weak. *You OK?* I ask, and after a long pause she says, *Nope.* She agrees to meet me at the dog run, and when she finally shows up nearly forty-five minutes late I see that she is, as she often is after using, still wearing her pajamas. She's got a sweatshirt over the tissue-thin, unwashed nightclothes, but I can see her collarbone jutting from her skin and her movements are labored. She looks as though she's lost ten pounds, and there weren't ten to lose. She has Essie's dog leash in one hand and a cigarette in the other, and when she sits down next to me I catch a strong whiff of alcohol, body odor, and cigarette smoke. I struggle not to react, but she's ripe and it's not easy to appear as if I don't notice.

How she smells is obviously the furthest thing from her mind. I've seen Polly after using a number of times, but something is different now. She seems startled by something more than the now familiar horror of having relapsed. I ask her what happened and she tells me that Heather came home with two eight balls Monday night and they used round the clock until Thursday night. On Friday, Heather's dealer comes by with another eight ball and the two of them dive in. After a few lines, Heather starts to complain of heart pains and lies down on the sofa. Polly is worried but does a few more lines. At some point, Heather passes out and Polly tries, unsuccessfully, to wake her up. She shakes her, splashes water on her face, and shouts her name, but nothing works. She checks for a pulse and feels Heather's heart beating in her chest so she knows she's alive. She must have overdosed, Polly realizes, as she does a big line to kill off her rising panic. When that doesn't work, she does another. There's almost an entire eight ball sitting on the coffee table, and when she thinks of calling the ambulance, she knows that when someone comes she'll have to go to the hospital with Heather. And stop using. She keeps doing line after line, thinking she's about to call 911, but each time the high doesn't last and soon she needs another line. She keeps thinking she'll call after one more. After two and a half hours or so of this, the eight ball is not gone, Heather is still unconscious, and Polly freaks out and finally calls 911. The paramedics come, get

Heather to the ER, pump her system clean, and she stays the night. Polly leaves Heather at the hospital once the doctor says she's going to be fine. She goes back to their apartment, finishes the eight ball, drinks vodka, and takes sleeping pills until she passes out. Late that morning, Heather comes home, and soon after that, I call. And here we are, in the dog park. *Something has to change,* she says, shaking her head. *I chose coke over my sister's life.*

Out of the blue, I remember a small rehab called High Watch in Kent, Connecticut, which is an old Twelve Step retreat that has meetings all day and is, I think I remember someone telling me once, cheap. On the park bench in the dog run we call information and get a person on the phone. There's a bed open on Monday and the daily rate is, with help from Polly's parents, manageable. She reserves the bed, commits to staying two weeks, and the next phone call is to my mother. Without giving it more than a moment's thought, I dial her number, and when she picks up I explain the situation. She agrees to meet us at the train station near Kent on Monday morning. When she asks if I'll spend the night, I lie and say that I have a commitment at a meeting that evening and need to return to the city. Between the phone call on the bench at the dog run and getting on the train Monday morning, Polly calls her parents and tells them what's been going on. It's the first they hear that she's been using drugs, and it's the first they hear that Heather has, too. They live in California and don't see their daughters very often. Somehow Polly's years of unemployment have not sounded alarm bells loud enough to make them think there is a serious problem. She asks them for help in paying the fee at the rehab and they agree. Of course there is a huge blowup with Heather, who denies everything to their parents and tells Polly that once she's left for rehab she can stay there or move back to California, but she's not welcome in her apartment anymore. Polly goes anyway.

We meet early Monday morning on the corner of Fifth Avenue and 14th Street, and Polly arrives with a small duffel bag. A friend has agreed to watch Essie, and as we get on the Metro North train to Wassaic, Polly says she hasn't been out of the city in three years. On the ride up, she tells me terrible but hilarious stories of getting smashed before teaching kindergarten and being completely bewildered when the other teachers at the school don't want to meet her around the corner for a drink on their lunch break. She, like me, has a few airport stories. One of the most vivid is one from her college years, when she leaves a bar one afternoon, hammered, and shows up at JFK airport with no idea where she is going to go, just that she's going somewhere, anywhere. She sees that a flight to Sarajevo is leaving later that night and books a ticket. She gets there with little money, just enough to sit in cafés all day and have drinks bought for her. *I sat there thinking I was so interesting, drinking in cafés in a country going to war. People were going off to die and I was feeling glamorous, fascinating. As if somehow the war had more to do with me than them.* Her story triggers a memory of my mother's battle with cancer. I remember telling friends that she was dying as I drank vodka after vodka, as if her sickness was impacting me more than her. I cringe with shame when I think about that time and, later, when I turned up at the hospital the day of her surgery after I'd been up the night before smoking crack.

We arrive at the Wassaic train station and the only car in the lot is my mother's. I can see her through the windshield of her Honda station wagon. Only when she steps out of the car toward the platform to greet us do I realize that I have not seen her in over a year. Six years since her radical mastectomy and five years since she completed a year of radiation treatments, her hair has returned, much thinner and lighter in color than before. As Polly gathers up her duffel bag and says heavily, *Here we go,* whatever difficulties I have with my mother don't matter.

The rehab is beautiful, which none of us expects. It looks like an expensive bed and breakfast one would go to for a weekend getaway from the city. The women who admit Polly are friendly and the place seems mostly empty. We walk across the property to where Polly will be sleeping, and as she puts her duffel on the bed, it only then occurs to me that she won't be in the city for two weeks. Two weeks with no dog run, no Polly. I have a flash of panic about relapsing, that without Polly around I'll somehow be less able to keep from picking up. I hope none of these thoughts register on my face as I hug Polly good-bye and walk glumly away as if I'm leaving my daughter at college. I want people to like her, worry she'll be lonely. *Call me if you need to, anytime,* I say pathetically as I leave her room to go.

My mother takes me back to the station to catch a train that leaves less than two hours after Polly and I arrived. As she drives, we don't talk about the silver or anything else that's been hard between us. She tells me that when I was in college she threw my father out of the house after a particularly ugly drunken scene. She agreed to let him come home only if he completed a stay at the rehab where we just left Polly, which, apparently, he did. I'm surprised by the story. I knew things had gotten bad between them while I was in college, that his drinking had escalated, but I had no idea that he'd gone to rehab. I listen as she describes how hard that time was, but I'm reluctant to get too engaged. I'm just now talking again with my father, after not speaking for nearly a decade, so I'm cautious about getting too deep into the old familiar dynamic of listening to my mother complain about him. My father is an early riser, always was, so over the last few weeks we've been talking in the mornings. I've been meeting Elliot at the tennis courts along the West Side Highway before he goes to work, so I get there early to reserve a court and call my father. It feels as if I am getting to know him for the first time on these calls. As my mother talks more about my father's drinking, I get more and more uncomfortable and eventually I change the subject.

We pull into the train station and wait awkwardly in the car. She asks about Polly's sister and The Library, tries, like any parent, to get a glimpse of her child's life. I answer vaguely, reluctant to include her in any of it, and eventually just say, *Thank you.* It is quiet in the car for some time. *I'm happy I could help, Billy. I'm just glad I can be of use,* she says tenderly as the train pulls up and I reach for the door. *Me, too,* I think as I kiss her on the cheek, leave the car, and go home.

# Goners

Jack asks me to meet him at a coffee shop on Irving Place. It's only a few blocks from my usual stomping grounds of Union Square, lower Fifth Avenue, and east Chelsea, but as I walk along the tall fences of Gramercy Park, it strikes me how small I've made the city again—how limited the terrain I travel, how predictable. As I'm about to cross up to Lexington from the top of the park I see a navy blue tracksuit with maroon stripes along the sleeves and pants. I see the tracksuit first and then the short, bearded, wiry, gold-ringed, Ray-Ban-clad kid wearing it. Lotto. Lotto is in lieu of Lowt, an old Jewish name given to Lotto by his old Jewish parents, who own and run a diamond store in the West 40s. Lotto was adopted as an infant, his parents are in their seventies, and he grew up in a town house on Gramercy Park that could double as an embassy. Last I heard he was at the Betty Ford Center in California. He's the kid I met over a year ago in Oregon at the rehab Noah and Kate sent me to. Then it was Lotto's ninth or tenth rehab. Now he's been to at least two more. In Oregon, Lotto resisted every suggestion, every instruction, and managed to alienate nearly every counselor and patient in the rehab. In clothes, language, and manner, he's hip-hop ghetto meets Italian mobster. He's the lippiest, most foul-mouthed, most confrontational kid I've ever met and also one of the funniest. In Oregon, we became friends. We'd walk the grounds of the rehab at night before curfew and he'd tell me stories of smuggling drugs into and busting out of therapeutic boarding schools up and down the east and west coasts. He was, then, twenty-one to my thirty-three. Now, both a year older and still, it seems—given that he's not at the Betty Ford Center, and I'm wearing shorts and a T-shirt on a weekday morning—not so much further along the road to recovery than when we last saw each other. I'd left the rehab in Oregon after completing five weeks in treatment; he left after going AWOL and secretly booking a ticket on my flight home to New York. *Surprise, surprise,* he had said at the airport, waving his boarding pass. *Time to get the hell home.*

Lotto spots me before I can say hi. *Yo, Billeeee!* he yells, more Gambino than Lansky. I notice that Lotto's wearing the usual amount of gold but less beard and that he's gained weight. He's graduated from whippet thin to wiry. His tracksuit, no doubt the smallest size made, still pools around his expensive running shoes and falls off his body like curtains. *You good?* he asks, and I say I'm just fine, that I have a few days sober and am making a run at ninety days. *Yo, I have ninety,* he says, *and I didn't need that joke rehab to get 'em. Really, Lotto?* I ask doubtfully. *Ninety?* He laughs and says, *Nah, but I will.*

I tell Lotto that I have to see my sponsor but he should meet me the next day at The Library. He gives me his new number—he's had two that I know of since we met in Oregon. Each rehab asks him to get rid of his old cell phone, as they did with me, so he doesn't have access to his dealers' numbers. We agree to see each other at The Library at 12:30 but it will be three days before I hear from him. *Let's get dinner,* he texts, and I suggest again that we meet at The Library. I don't hear from him for a few days, so when he texts and suggests dinner again, I agree to meet him at a place in the far West Village—more of a lounge than a restaurant. When I get there he's with three girls. All blond, all look like they're in high school, all talking on or texting from their cell phones. *Looks like a party,* I say as I sit down, and Lotto smirks and says, *What else is new?* The girls are drinking champagne—*Of course they are,* I think. Lotto has a large bottle of Pellegrino in front of him. *Bubbly?* he jokes as he holds up the bottle. I nod yes and gesture toward the girls. He introduces me and they barely look up from their gadgets. A waiter comes, we order whatever we order, and when the girls all leave for the bathroom, Lotto tells me he's in love. *She's a good girl,* he says, and I ask which one of the three she is and he says, *Oh no, not these bitches, they're just friends. Tess is in art school and is in the studio tonight working on some sculpture or installation or something.* I ask him where he met her and he tells me the story of how he spotted her at Barneys, followed her out onto Madison Avenue, and asked her to dinner. I try to picture the scene and have a hard time seeing how Lotto pulls off this kind of move, but then again he has three girls at dinner tonight so who knows. *You'd like her, Billy,* he says seriously. *I know you would.*

The food finally arrives and the girls return from the bathroom looking a little more awake than before they left, which is my cue to eat quickly, throw a few twenties on the table, and go. I tell Lotto to meet me at the 12:30 the next day, that we can get coffee after. He gets up and extends his hand in the way that all young straight boys do these days. I ignore his hand and give him a hug instead. *Be good,* I say into his ear. *And meet me tomorrow.*

To my great surprise, he does—at 1:30, on the bottom step of The Library. I see him as I'm leaving to grab a coffee before going back to the two o'clock. Tracksuit, Ray-Bans, gold necklace, cigarette. He's just a kid but he looks like a sixty-year-old casino lizard from Atlantic City. *Where's my coffee?* he says laughing and starts walking to University before I even say hello.

Lotto tells me all about Tess. How she grew up all over the world, how her father is some kind of diplomat. He drops the names of a few very famous people who he says are to Tess *practically family.* Lotto hits his stride when famous people come into the picture. There is almost never a story that doesn't somehow come around to a celebrity. From the socialites he went to the therapeutic boarding schools with *(whores)* to the athletes who shop at the diamond store his parents own *(whoremasters)* to the rap stars who frequent the parties he goes to *(masters of all whoremasters)*—there are famous people. And always they are described as friends or practically family. This story is no different. But one difference is how he talks about this girl. She, too, has been to rehab, it turns out. *She just gets me,* he says, and shrugs. I ask if she goes to meetings of any kind and he says that she's figured out a way to use a little heroin on the weekends and not drink at all. *Booze was her problem, not drugs,* he says seriously. *And since heroin is not my thing, there's no temptation for me.* I listen to him and for a minute think he's joking. When I realize he's not, I tell him he's out of his mind. *We're good for each other,* he argues. *She keeps me away from coke and I keep her away from booze. She's getting an MFA and we're going to open a gallery together in Soho with my cousin Sam.* I honestly don't know where to begin; his earnestness is so palpable that I can't bear to say anything beyond suggesting we head back to The Library to catch the two o'clock meeting. *We can make it,* I say like a parent trying to make homework or going to the dentist sound like fun. Lotto's face pinches and by some miracle he actually follows me back to the meeting.

Lotto and I trade phone calls over the next few days. He says he'll show up at meetings but never does. He leaves a long message one night and tells me how glad he is we're friends, that we're in each other's lives, that it's fate that we should be on this journey together, and I know from the charged sentimental urgency in his voice that he's high. This is the last message I get for a week. And then, the day after taking Polly to Connecticut, while I'm doing laundry in the basement of my building, I get a call from his mother. Something has happened, she says, and could I come over to their house right away. It's late afternoon and I had been planning to go to the Meeting House at six. But instead I immediately start walking over to Gramercy Park. On the way, Lotto's mother, who sounds as exhausted and bewildered as I've ever heard anyone sound, tells me what happened. Four nights before, Lotto and his younger cousin Sam were in his bedroom. Lotto had a bag of cocaine and Sam apparently wanted to try it. Lotto, according to his mother, tried to persuade him not to but he was persistent. So Lotto cuts him a line and within minutes Sam has a seizure and is soon unconscious. They call 911, and by the time the ambulance arrives he is dead. Apparently he'd taken several antianxiety medications that day, and combined with cocaine they caused his heart to fail. The family—Lotto's father's brother—had to be called and they and the police have agreed it's a no-fault fatality. Lotto's mother is telling me all this because they want him to enter a year-long treatment program in Northern California, some place a consultant they hired has strongly recommended. Lotto is, she says, refusing to go and threatening to kill himself.

I arrive at Gramercy Park just as Lotto's mother is finishing the story and ask her to remind me what the address is. *Yep, that's the one,* I mutter to myself as I look up at the enormous place. I expect Lotto's mother to greet me at the door, but instead it's Lotto. I had imagined him looking strung out, red-eyed, and shaky from all that's gone on and by his mother's description. But he's freshly showered, shaved (for once), and in jeans and polo shirt. I barely recognize him without the tracksuit, sunglasses, and beard, and see, for the first time, that underneath Lotto's usual costume, he's handsome. *Maybe this is what the girls see in him,* I think, and not just the cash and access to clubs and parties. Lotto gives me a hug and apologizes for his mother's calling. We go to the kitchen and he sits on the counter and starts talking.

Whatever grief Lotto feels is hidden behind a head of combed hair, a clean shave, and a steely tone. *I didn't know,* he says over and over again. *I didn't know.* His cousin didn't seem high, he says, didn't seem like he was on anything. *Who knew about the medications!?!? Jesus!* he bellows, his composure now gone. Lotto tells me that when Sam bullied him into trying a line of coke he didn't think it was such a big deal. *How was I supposed to know? HOW?!?* he yells across the kitchen. *How the fuck is this my fault!??! And now my mother has you up in my shit. Billy, don't even try to talk me into going to rehab. There aren't any left to go to!*

For a moment, as I run down the list of rehabs I know he's been in and out of, I think he may be right. *Have you been to this one in Northern California your mom has lined up?* I ask, genuinely not knowing the answer. *No,* he says, *but it's a fucking cash machine like all the rest. You put the druggie in and they take the cash out. And there is no way I'm going for a year. No. Fucking. Way.* He tells me how his mother has called Tess and told her Lotto has left town, that he's in treatment again and not to call. Tess, in turn, texts Lotto that she needs to step away. *Too much drama,* she writes. *BITCH!!* he shouts. He punctuates what he's yelling with a refrain that goes something like *I'm going to walk out this fucking door and find a fucking gun and blow my fucking brains out before I go to rehab again.* It goes on like this for over an hour, and when I start thinking of Lotto in the city, shame-saddled with his cousin's death, heartbroken and suicidal, I think, *He won't live.* Which is what I say. *You're not going to live.* I tell him that he's going to be dead just like his cousin — not by a gun, which we both know he's not going to get, but by an overdose. And as I say this I remember Lotto on one of our evening walks in Oregon. He is describing his group of friends in high school standing on a corner in the Bronx trying to score weed, *Freezing our hairless balls off, all of us wearing these big puffy North Face jackets — blue, red, green, purple — we looked like a pack of Skittles.* He says this out of the corner of his mouth, deadpan, a smartass twenty-one-year-old sounding like an old Catskills comedian warming up a room. I remember him showing up at the airport in Portland a year ago, waving his boarding pass, how excited and lonely and lost he seemed. And here he is, lost again, trying to put a tough face on a horrible tragedy, trying to call the shots when his world, by his own hand, has fallen apart once more. I start crying. It's the first cry in months, the first one since I walked out the door of my life five months ago, since that relapse that sent me headlong into a two-month suicide dive. I had, then, walked out the door and into the city like Lotto is about to do. *I'm looking at someone who is about to be dead,* I keep thinking, and then I think of his cousin Sam, whom I never met but heard a dozen stories about. Sam was two years younger than Lotto, an on-again, off-again partner in crime since elementary school who somehow never got in trouble or took things as far as Lotto did. Sam did well enough in high school to go to a cushy four-year liberal arts college in Florida, where he had just finished his sophomore year. This kid who, from a distance, had a better chance than Lotto of making something of his life is now dead. *We die,* I think. *That's what we do. Whether we want to or not that's where this goes.* I think of Polly doing lines during Heather's overdose. I think of me, less than two weeks ago, going to get lighters to do enough drugs to jump off a seventeen-story terrace. Polly, Heather, Lotto, me — we don't stand a chance. *You don't stand a chance,* I blubber through tears at Lotto. *You don't stand a chance unless you go. You're going to end up just like Sam. Or you're going to kill someone else you love and end up in jail.* Lotto doesn't move or speak, just sits on that sleek stainless steel counter.

Lotto's mother comes in. She gets me a tissue to wipe my eyes, but I can't stop sobbing. If you only cry once every few years, it's not pretty. This was not pretty. *Are you OK?* she asks, and I say, pointing to Lotto, *I will be if he goes to California.*

And he does. Though I'd like to think my tear-streaked speech in the kitchen is what pushed him to make the right decision, I learn later from his mother that she and Lotto's father threatened—convincingly this time—to throw him out, cut him off entirely, and let him fend for himself if he didn't go, and stay, for a whole year. He texts me the next morning: *Going to Cali. Wish me luck, brother.*

The next night, I relapse. Polly is still in rehab, Lotto will be tucked away in his eleventh or twelfth rehab in Napa Valley, and I'll be coming home from the Meeting House, thinking about Noah, work, money, all the things Jack has counseled me to stop thinking and worrying and grieving about. And then I think about getting high. I think about it and then I do it. It's after midnight when I call Rico. I use the occasion to pay him back the thousand dollars I owe him and buy a bag of crack. I smoke it down and at two in the morning go to Mark's. He's there with three other people—two middle-aged guys and a kid in his early twenties. I sleep with all of them and smoke their drugs, since I have reached my ATM limit and have access to no more money. *My, my, how the mighty have fallen,* Mark cracks when he returns to his bedroom to survey the scene. And I think, *I've always been down here, it's just more obvious now.*

I leave Mark's around noon, crawl into bed, blast the air-conditioning, and take a fistful of Tylenol PM. Polly leaves a message from the pay phone at High Watch. She's going to meetings all day and night, she says, and the food is good. She misses Heather and Essie and me but she'll be home soon. Heather, who has calmed down and called Polly to say she can still live in the apartment, is renting a car and picking her up next Monday. *I'm comin' home, Crackhead. You better be sober.*

I don't tell Polly or anyone else, including Jack, about the relapse. I keep it a secret, just like I used to with Noah. I think

I'm doing it for her and not me. I think it's some kind of sacrifice so she doesn't begin to get the idea that staying sober is impossible. I don't want her to think what I'm beginning to suspect: that none of what works for Jack and Asa and Luke and Annie is going to work for me. I'm like Lotto, without the wealth, without the endless safety nets of rehab after rehab. I'm like Sam and like I imagine Lotto would be if he hadn't left for California: a goner.

# Done

First Monday in June. Polly's two weeks in rehab are up and Heather brings her back to the city in time for the two o'clock meeting. She comes in just before it starts and sits down across from me. She looks younger, brighter. I'm so used to seeing Polly in her pajamas or in unwashed sweat-pants and T-shirts that it's jarring to see her in clean jeans and a blouse, her hair washed and skin clear. At the break, when Polly raises her hand and announces that she has seventeen days, the place goes wild. Later, when she shares about her time away, Pam and others sob and sigh with what can only be described as joy.

At the dog run afterward, Polly tells me that Heather has promised to slow down, and if she uses, not to use in the apartment. Polly seems hopeful, but I can't help but doubt that whatever promises Heather has made she will surely break. And soon. Now that Polly has some clean days together, I look on the bright side and think maybe we're both out of the woods, finally. I haven't told her about my relapse and don't plan to.

Our schedule of the 12:30, two o'clock, and dog run resumes. Jack has insisted that I take a service commitment at a meeting, so I make coffee and set up the chairs at the Meeting House on Wednesday nights. There's another guy who shares the commitment with me—a gentle fellow in his early forties whose story is very different from mine. His story reminds me of my father's—years of drinking and a slow, steady narrowing of a life until the loneliness causes enough agony to instigate change. For my father, it wasn't until his mid-sixties, when he was living alone in a small house in New Hampshire, twice divorced, with children who didn't speak to him and friends and siblings who had, one by one, gradually disappeared. What is bewildering to me is that my father didn't get sober—instead he switched from scotch to beer—but he still went through the kind of change that I see happen in the people who do. It began, at least from what I can tell, with a young couple who lived nearby. Dad got to know the husband because he also had a small plane at the nearby landing strip. One thing leads to another, and the couple invite my dad over for dinner. Sometime soon after the dinner, the wife is diagnosed with a serious cancer and given less than a year to live. They find out that there are experimental treatments that take place in Boston and all of a sudden their lives are in chaos. Whether he offered or they asked I don't know, but my father begins watching their dog—a poodle, of all things—while they are away. He gets very attached to the dog and it begins to stay over at his place for longer and longer stretches. As the wife becomes weak from the treatments, she is no longer able to drive herself to Boston for her frequent doctor's appointments. The husband is a commercial airline pilot, as my dad had been, so there are many times when he is simply not available to drive her. My father steps in and begins driving. This goes on for several years until, eventually, the woman dies. I remember my father mentioning the couple and their tragic situation during one of the first conversations we have when I'm back in New York from White Plains. By this time, her death was near. I remember being baffled by and jealous of his instinctive care for these strangers, particularly since, until now, he's had very little to do with my life or with any of my three siblings. My father and I speak two or three times a week that spring and summer, and there isn't one time when he doesn't mention these people or their poodle, which I think has basically become his. Before this, conversations with my father usually involved patiently listening to him complain about the president (it never matters which one), Congress, the health care industry, or an old favorite, the Kennedys. But now, most of the whipping boys have vanished. Not all, but most. In their place are detailed accounts of this woman's decline, the toll on her husband, and the latest attempt to reverse what appears to be irreversible. And questions. About my days, how I fill them, and recent developments with Polly and Asa and Jack, all of whom I've described to him in detail, the first people in my life since grammar school I've talked about with him or even mentioned. During this time he also becomes increasingly involved with my younger siblings, whose twenties are drawing to a bumpy close. He makes sure they have insurance, lawyers for legal troubles, money for night classes. And my nephews, his grandsons—he attends every birthday in Maine, flies his small plane to recitals and sporting events even. It doesn't happen overnight, but phone call by phone call, action by action, he becomes part of our lives, a member of the family—the father, the grandfather and friend he never was. That he still drinks, albeit far less than before, is none of my business (Jack's phrase, not mine).

The Wednesday setting-up-the-meeting commitment takes all of twenty minutes before the meeting, and yet I bring it up in every conversation, every description about my routine, every discussion about getting sober. People who address the United Nations or perform open heart surgery no doubt talk less about what they do than I did about those twenty minutes of flipping light switches, brewing coffee, and arranging chairs once a week. After tennis in the mornings with Elliot, or at dinner with Jean at Basta Pasta, I go on and on. I even tell them about the commitments I don't have yet. After ninety days, Jack says, I need to chair a meeting. There are ten different meetings a week at The Library—speaker meetings, topic meetings, meditation meetings, et cetera— and I wonder and worry about which one I'll get and if I'll be confident enough to sit in front of the group and lead. Whenever I try to talk to Jack about this stuff he cuts the conversation short with *Worry about which one when it's time. Get ninety days, and then let's talk about it.* So until then, it's mostly Jean and Elliot and, amazingly, my father who I talk to about this stuff. And, of course, Polly.

Only a few days after Polly returns home, Heather starts using in the apartment again. And more people than before seem to be using with her there. Polly shares about what's going on in meetings and talks to me about it at the dog run, but she still can't imagine moving out. Not only does she not think she can afford to move, but also she's worried that if she does, Heather will overdose, either accidentally or on purpose. In the last few days, when the subject of moving out comes up, Heather has threatened to kill herself if Polly leaves. It's a strange development, since less than a month ago Heather was demanding Polly move out, but as Annie reminds me one afternoon over coffee, Heather is losing her running buddy. Polly is getting sober and Heather isn't, and Heather's mad. That they are twins is easy to forget. Heather is stocky whereas Polly is rail thin. Heather has a coiled, angry energy that seems as if it could spring and strike at any moment. Polly is someone who looks more likely to hurt herself than anyone or anything else. Polly has Greenpeace and PETA stickers on her knapsack. Heather has a skull tattooed on the back of her neck. I know how difficult it is getting sober on my own, but living with a using buddy—and a twin, no less—who has dealers and drug addicts in and out of the apartment is unimaginable. Polly may have talked about it, but it's only now that I'm really beginning to recognize how tough what she's trying to do is. *That Heather is a strong undertow,* Annie says. *It's a good thing Polly was a champion swimmer in college.*

Polly keeps sharing about Heather, keeps showing up to meetings, and continues to walk dogs in the neighborhood to cover her portion of the rent. May winds down and as it does I think, *These have been the longest two months of my life.* Not because they've been the hardest but because it seems that so much has happened, so many new people have come into my life, and even more have left. I'm hopeful but I'm also tired. I didn't count on relapsing when I first came back to the city from White Plains. Didn't count on how expensive those relapses would be. Money is tight. With the last relapse and money needed for one of the lawyers handling my settlement with Kate, I've wiped out what would have paid June's rent. I'm trying to sell the only Eggleston photograph that's of any value in a portfolio I have, but so far have had no luck. Dave's friend, a respected art dealer, is doing her best—as a favor to Dave—to unload at least that one, but there have been no bites. On the bright side, an envelope arrives with a preapproved credit card and, on a lark, I send back the papers with a signature and a few weeks later a credit card appears with a $17,000 line of credit. From a cash advance that I get with this card I pay the June rent. It takes a number of visits to the ATM to advance that much cash from the credit card, and when I finally have $2,500 I deposit the money in my checking account and write a check to the landlord. *One more month of shelter,* I think, as I drop the envelope in the mailbox, and I'm genuinely grateful as I do.

During, in between, and after my meetings, I still think
about getting high, still get cravings. I make my phone
calls, share at The Library about it, but still feel as if I'm
a sitting duck. Less than two weeks after my last relapse,
I pick up again. It's like all the other times. A memory of
getting high, a sudden craving, the world narrowing to one
desire. I can't remember much about that day, the events
or thoughts preceding the phone call to Happy. I remember using alone and then not alone. Someone I don't know
materializes, the way these people, these people precisely
like me, always do. We run out. It's nine in the morning.
He says he has a connection uptown. I give him two hundred dollars, he leaves and doesn't return. It's a long, grim
day and I scrape the stems and screens that I have, smoke
them until they resemble charcoal, and eventually give up.
There are a few beers left in the refrigerator. I drink one
down, take a few Tylenol PMs, and lie in bed and wait until Happy or Rico turns his phone on. There is no doubt
in my mind that I will call to get more. I can get a few
hundred dollars from the credit card I advanced the rent
money from. It's mid-afternoon and the sun is pulsing on
the other side of the drawn blinds. The old sheet nailed to
the wall above the terrace door flaps with the air gushing
from the wheezing air conditioner.

I wait, fall asleep for a little while, wake up at seven or eight, and even though I know the dealers are open for business again, I don't call them. Later, I think. I'm exhausted. There's a phrase I hear in the rooms all the time — *Sick and tired of being sick and tired* — and it couldn't diagnose more acutely how I feel. I go out to the terrace, look down to 15th Street, and again think about jumping. *Why do I always want to die?* I think impatiently. I always have, as long as I can remember, and never as much as when I'm coming down from a high, nearing the ruin of consequences that wait. It's so predictable, so selfish, and so weak. I go back inside and down the last beer — an Amstel Light, of all things. It doesn't feel like an end but it will be. Perhaps not *the* end, but *an* end.

I sleep through the night without waking and begin the day as I've done most days since April. I go to the gym, get to the 12:30 meeting early, raise my hand, and count one day for the last time. I don't remember who is there that day, but I do remember staying for the two o'clock and, after, going to the dog run with Polly. The dogs race in circles, hump each other, bark. The guys in the tracksuits make their phone calls and we sit in the middle of it all, me with one day and she with over three weeks. *Look who's on top now, Crackhead,* she teases, and I laugh, for what feels like the very first time.

Later in the summer, a month after Polly is back from rehab, The Library closes for a day. It's a Monday and the closing is either for a holiday or for a renovation of some kind. Polly and I agree to meet at Dean & Deluca at noon for a coffee and then walk east to a meeting at one o'clock. Walking up University I can see Polly sitting on a stool in the window. Before I get to the door I know something's wrong. There is the angle of her slouch, her hair falling in her face, and the surest sign of all: her pajamas. *Motherfucker,* I say or think and rush inside. *Motherfuckingmotherfucker!* I shout as I get closer and see for sure that she's a wreck, that she's been using. *Are you kidding me?* I ask as I approach her on the stool. Usually when Polly relapses I react in the way she usually reacts with me—with disappointment, fear, even, but always with compassion, and always quick with a plan to get to a meeting.

This time I'm furious. But not as furious as I am when she says, *I'm giving up. Sobriety isn't for me. I had a long talk with Heather this morning and it's what I decided.* I cannot believe what I'm hearing. *HEATHER?!!??* I bellow. *Are you kidding? You're now taking advice from Heather?* She just looks at me. It's not a conversation. She's barely in front of me now. She's already back in the apartment. Of course she looks terrible, of course she hasn't slept all night. But what she's saying is not part of the script. She's supposed to get back on the horse, go to a meeting with me right away, and announce that she has one day. *I'm done,* she says, more matter-of-fact than defiant. *I'm sorry, but I'm done.* I don't know what to say. We sit in the window and stare at each other and two things cross my mind: (1) I'm jealous that when we leave she will return to an apartment just a few blocks away to drugs, and (2) I'm sure she's going to die. Not someday, not even soon, but now, today, right after we part ways. I know she's going to die and I know that there is nothing I can do about it. She's not as strong as Heather is, not as tough, can't do the kinds of drugs she does. Do I call the police to raid Heather's apartment? Is it better for her to be in jail than to be dead? What if Noah had done that with me? I'd be in jail now. But am I now so much better off? If I'd gone to jail I'd probably have a lot more than a few weeks sober by now. And then, right there, before I say another word, I pray. Jack is always telling me to pray and when I balk he usually just says, *Whatever you're doing isn't working, so you might as well try.* So now, for Polly, I do. To whom or to what I don't know, but to something: *Tell me what to say. Tell me what to say so she doesn't die. Please.* But no words come and I eventually say what my friend Lili said to me months ago after she found me deep in a bender at One Fifth: *You want to die, die. You want to live, call me. But until then, leave me out of it.* And just as I say these same words, Polly's up off the stool, out the door, and back on the street. She's gone. Just like that.

I go to the meeting in the East Village and the only one there I know is Pam. I raise my hand, announce my day count, and wonder if Polly doesn't have the right idea. After the meeting I tell Pam what's happened and she just shakes her head in her sanguine, maternal way and says, *Sometimes you have to let them go so that they can come back. In the meantime, you pray they don't die.*

After the East Village meeting I go home, fall asleep, and the next day can't bear to go to the 12:30 meeting. *But what if Polly's there?* I think, and rush out the door to get to The Library on time. Polly's not there. I stay for the two o'clock and Polly doesn't show. She doesn't turn up at the Meeting House either. For the next few weeks I go to every meeting, hoping she'll appear. I see her once, on the street. She's coming up Fifth Avenue, walking Essie and smoking a cigarette. She's in her sweatpants, all angles and jutting bones, moving at a snail's pace. She looks like the Grim Reaper's girlfriend. We cross each other on the sidewalk and when I say hi she puts her hand up to wave me away. I keep going.

Asa tells me to pull back and let Polly hit her bottom. Jack and Annie and Luke do, too. But what if her bottom is death? What if there is something I can do that could keep her from dying? At one point Asa recommends I go to an Al-Anon meeting. *I drive people into those meetings,* I joke. *I don't actually go there myself.* Asa shakes his head.

Life goes on, my one day becomes a few days and then a few weeks. There is a night after dinner on Sixth Avenue when I say good-bye to Cy and look down toward Houston and wonder what Mark is up to. I walk down into the trigger zone and stand on the corner of Sixth and Houston and see that his lights are on. Shadows pass in front of the window and my heart races as I conjure scenarios of what is transpiring there. As if I have to imagine. The same thing is always transpiring there. I cross Sixth Avenue, cross down to the south side of Houston, and step toward the building. *Fuck it,* I think, like I always do at this moment, and head toward the door. But before I press the buzzer, I think of Polly. What if she calls me when I'm in there? What if she hears I've relapsed again? What if I don't make it to the meeting tomorrow, stay up for a few days, and miss her when she comes back in? What if my picking up gives her another excuse to keep using? It's narcissistic, I realize as I'm thinking it, but I can't help but ask myself: *What if my picking up results in Polly dying?* The logic is suddenly so plausible, so powerful, and so likely that it stops me in my tracks. It stops me less than ten feet from the buzzer I've pressed countless times over too many years and with the same grim results. I've never been this close and not gone in.

I turn around and start walking north on Sixth Avenue, away from Mark's, where I never set foot again. I call Jack and leave a message on his voice mail. I tell him I've gone into the trigger zone and come out clean.

Over the next few weeks there are a dozen or so times when the thought to call Happy or Rico or go to Mark's happens in the way that it always has. The idea sparks and with it a craving to use and then the plans to figure out how I can. Each of these times I think of Polly or Lotto or someone in the rooms counting days who I've given my number to, and each of these times I stop long enough to call either Jack or Asa or Annie, and by the time I do the urge passes. And then, miraculously, the cravings disappear. The thoughts still come— I expect they always will—but the craving doesn't follow. The desire to use or drink vanishes as stealthily as it used to arrive. I won't even notice it go, just that it has.

# Pink Cloud

It's the Fourth of July and Elliot and I go for a hike on Bear Mountain. We hike and walk for a few hours and find our way to a ridge that looks south down the Hudson River to Manhattan. *It looks like Oz,* Elliot says as the ridge of buildings appears, floating on the horizon like a crown. I remember thinking the same thing in Dave's car three months ago on the drive from White Plains. That car ride now seems a lifetime away.

Elliot and I return to the city just as it's getting dark. The elevator man, the older of the two brothers, is smiling when we enter the lobby and we ask why. *The roof is open!* he says loudly, as if we should know why this is cause for celebration. *For the fireworks!* Of course, the fireworks, the Fourth of July. We get off the elevator on the twentieth floor and rush to the roof. The building is the last tall building on Seventh Avenue before the acres of town houses and low buildings of the West Village begin to spread south of 14th Street, so the view from the roof is breathtaking. We see the long lit riverbanks of New Jersey, the huddled buildings that make up what's left of the financial district, the Met Life tower north of the Flatiron, and the tallest of all, the Empire State Building, celebrating in red, white, and blue lights. Never has the city looked so festive, so possible. Fireworks begin to explode up and down the Hudson River, south of Battery Park, and across town above the East River. I have never seen so many fireworks at once, and the two of us stand there, stunned. We kiss. Not for the first time since our affair several years ago and not for the first time that day, but in a way that makes it clear that something is beginning, or has begun and is now being acknowledged. It is one of the great kisses of my life. Jack warned me against getting involved romantically until I had ninety days, but it's a suggestion I fail to take. The worry is that if there is heartbreak or romantic upset in those ninety days, one will relapse over it. Maybe because my heart was already broken, and Elliot came in like a friend and stayed as something more, it was different. I

don't know. I wouldn't recommend it to anyone else, but I
also don't regret it.

Two days after the Fourth of July, I arrange to meet Asa at
Mary Ann's, a Mexican restaurant in Chelsea. Oddly, it's the
restaurant my girlfriend Marie took me to on our first trip to
New York together, the summer after I graduated from college. When I go to the bathroom I look in the mirror that
could well be the same mirror I looked at all those years ago.
Twenty-one then, thirty-four now; jobless then, jobless now,
I think, and then say to my reflection, *Nothing's changed*. I
look closer and see the creep of wrinkles around my eyes and
along my brow, and the more-than-a-few gray hairs above.
Some things *have* changed, I think, and then again as I return
to the table and see two glasses of tap water.

I've asked Asa to dinner to tell him about Elliot. I'm nervous
because I know he has developed feelings for me. I know this
because he told me so a few weeks earlier—after a meeting,
in my apartment—before he kissed me. I kissed him right
back and for a little while, we kissed. It was a mistake, I knew
it, but it felt good, and as with all the other mistakes that
felt good, I had no power to stop this one before the damage
was done. Asa had become my life raft and I had clung too

tightly. I called him all the time, followed him from meeting to meeting, talked his ear off, and only now had begun to listen. After the kiss, I told him I didn't and never would have romantic feelings for him and that I was sorry if I'd led him to believe otherwise. *And let's face it,* I pointed out, trying to make light of the event but also reminding him of the obvious, *I'm hardly a catch. Among other things, I have less than three weeks sober and I can't stop relapsing.*

What I said didn't matter. Our relationship was never the same again. By then, Luke, Polly, Annie, and a few other people from the rooms had come into my life. Jack had, for weeks, perhaps expecting this very thing, encouraged me to spend time with and call people other than Asa. *Spread the neediness,* he said. *There's plenty to go around.* And I did.

After the food arrives, I tell Asa about Elliot. The Fourth of July hike, the rooftop fireworks, the kiss, the whole shebang. *So you're seeing him now? He's your boyfriend? Is that what this is about?* he asks, gesturing to the burritos, the nachos, the restaurant. As I say yes, Asa pushes his chair back, crosses the dining room, and shoots out the door. I chase after him but he waves me away, shakes his head, and disappears down 16th Street. By this point I have lost a lot of

people—clients, friends, colleagues, Noah—but watching
Asa rush down the street away from me is one of the tough-
est losses. I didn't, and still don't, have anything to compare
it to. How do you thank someone for saving your life? How
do you apologize for needing him too much? For not being stronger when it mattered? If I had the words I would
have said them. But that night I have only his name, which
I shout uselessly as he hurries down 16th Street, his red hair
and pale skin disappearing into the night like they had the
first night we met.

Not long after, I get a phone call from Dave's art dealer.
There is an offer for the Eggleston photograph she is trying
to sell for me, and it's for what she's asking. Even better, she
thinks she has a buyer for two more, and even though their
value is a bit less, the prospect of those two selling as well is
like winning the lottery. With less than a thousand left in my
bank account, and tens of thousands of dollars now piled up
on credit cards, the timing of her phone call couldn't be better. She eventually sells all three, and with that money I am
able to stay in the 15th Street apartment.

Annie and I go to Coney Island. Neither of us has been
there before, and it's the day of the annual Mermaid Parade.

We eat the creamiest, most delicious gelato imaginable and watch guys in drag and girls who look like guys in drag prance and jiggle on and alongside floats made of everything from macaroni to marshmallows. On the ride home we sit down next to a woman who moves, dramatically and with great sighing, to the end of the subway car bench. When she's not looking, Annie mimics her gesture and it is, this little impromptu impersonation, the funniest thing I have ever seen. We laugh so hard the woman leaves the car at the next station and we howl all the way back to the city. Later that night it occurs to me that I haven't thought about drinking or using in weeks. I open a journal I've been keeping since White Plains and write: *Coney Island with Annie today. No cravings for weeks. How did this happen?*

Before the summer is over, almost two months since that grim day in Dean & Deluca, Polly calls. It's morning and I haven't left for the gym yet. At first, I think I'm imagining her name on the screen of my cell phone—I have so many times. I pick up. She asks me to meet her at the dog run, and I say I'll leave immediately. I peel out the door and run down 15th Street, past Sixth Avenue, past Fifth, all the way to Union Square. I manage to call Jack as I huff and puff toward the dog run and leave an excited message. And, like the last time I saw Polly and a few other times since, I pray.

To whatever forces have kept me sober this long, I pray for
the right words. *TELL ME WHAT TO SAY!* I yell as I run.
*Please.*

I arrive at the dog run and Polly is sitting on our usual bench.
Essie is waddling nearby. I don't need any words because
she has the ones that matter. *I need help,* she says, not looking particularly hungover or strung out, just tired. *Will you
take me to a meeting?* she asks. *Are you kidding?* I answer. *I've
been waiting my whole life.* And though the words are lazy and
said playfully, as I say them I know they're true. I know in
that instant that everything that has happened—every last
lucky, lonely, destructive, delusional, selfish, wretched, insane, desperate second of it—has made this moment on the
bench with Polly possible. I'm sober enough to show up, addict enough to be asked. I'm one of her kind and she's one
of mine and there is no one in the world who can help us but
each other. I tell her about the night on Houston and Sixth
Avenue in front of Mark's apartment, how I stepped away
and she was the reason. *Nah, Crackhead, it would take a hell
of a lot more than me to keep you from the pipe.* We laugh, the
way addicts laugh about the agony of their using in the only
way that makes it bearable: with each other.

Soon after that morning, Polly and I move all of her belongings into a truck driven by a scruffy cute guy from the rooms, someone neither Polly nor I know. Polly shares in a meeting that she's moving and that she needs a truck, and this guy materializes and offers not only his truck and his driving skills but his hands and back as well. He and I spend hours shoving boxes and chairs and bookcases into the small one-bedroom apartment in Astoria Polly finds on Craigslist.

Heather comes by while we are moving Polly out and without a word walks in and out of the apartment, around the truck, and alongside us as we haul bags and furniture down the hall and into the street. I worry she is going to let me have it before we're finished, but just before the three of us pile into the truck, she turns to me and says without looking me in the eye, *Thank you.* Tailgate shut, Polly jammed in the front seat between me and the cute guy driving, we start to roll down St. Mark's Place. *Wait!* Polly shouts. *I forgot something in the apartment.* Before the truck comes to a stop, she is nudging me to let her out. I hesitate, afraid she's changed her mind, that once she gets out she'll never get back in. *C'mon, it's just gonna take a minute,* she says, more wistful than impatient. I let her out and watch as she keys the lock to the building door and disappears inside. Something unfamiliar plays on the radio and the stranger next to me taps the wheel. Minutes pass and my eyes are closed when Polly climbs in next to me. She's shaking, her eyes are red from crying, and there is nothing in her hands retrieved from the apartment. *Go,* she croaks-more-than-speaks. *Before I change my mind, go.* And so we do. It takes most of the afternoon to move Polly into her new apartment. Neither of us ever sees the cute, generous guy again.

On the last night of summer, at the end of Labor Day weekend, Elliot and I play tennis. It's a beautiful night—crisp, clear, and the sky is crowded with clouds that look like enormous waves crashing against a shore. After we play, we walk up the West Side Highway to the pier and collapse on the grass. The sky turns pink above us. The air is chilly and the green and red lights of New Jersey blink across the water. As the sun dips lower, the pink darkens against the clouds, and everything—the city, the river, the people around us—appears to shrink against the magnificent sky. Neither of us speaks. In a few minutes it will be dark. In the morning, summer will be over. I am happy, I think—for the first time in my life, happy. I'm sober, surrounded day and night by other sober people, the urge to drink and use has left, finally; I have just enough money in the bank to pay the rent and send tiny checks to the many people and places I owe, and I'm with someone I have no secrets from. *I wish I could stop time*, I tell Elliot. *If I could, I would stop it right now, under this great pink cloud.* We shiver in our damp tennis clothes and huddle into each other for warmth. *I know*, Elliot whispers into the darkening night. *Wouldn't it be wonderful.*

# Shoulder to Shoulder

On a Sunday night in September, I raise my hand in a meeting and say that I have ninety days. It is at the Meeting House, and Polly and Jack are there. Luke and Annie are there, too, along with a few other people from The Library. Though I have left messages to tell him when and where and asking him to please come, Asa is not. At midnight that night, when the Empire State Building turns its lights off as it always does, it is officially a new day, and the day after that another and the day after that another and so on and so on until a year, and then another and then another and then four, and as I write this now—five years, eight months, and two days. And with the help of the rooms, the people in them, and the power their words and actions and courage have shown me—a power that is unquestionably greater than myself, greater than my desire to use, to drink, and to die—tomorrow will, likely, be one day more.

Before the end of the year, Jean invites me to a party. It's a dinner for someone important, and it's large and seated and in her apartment. Jean's had lots of parties since I've come back to New York, and with each one she has said, *Don't worry, it'll be a bore anyway,* but with this one she says, over dinner at Basta Pasta, that she wants me to come, that her daughters are coming and that she'd like me to be there. Of course I say yes. The dinner is a month away, and I worry about it from the moment she asks. All my outings with Jean this year—theater, music, movies—have been one-on-one, and the few suppers at her apartment have been in the kitchen, with Paul, her chef, cooking and chatting behind the counter. I haven't been to one party or social function that hasn't been a sober gathering of people from the rooms, or a small group of very close, very supportive friends. It's only when I think about going to this party at Jean's that I recognize fully how protected these months have been, how sealed off. Jean's parties, even on a good day, are not for the faint of heart. But as a first outing, after hiding inside a sober cocoon for half a year, it is downright terrifying. I keep imagining people asking one question: *What do you do?* And when I imagine what I say in response, I come up with nothing. *I was in book publishing, and now....* In the rooms it's not uncommon for people to be out of work or taking time off to get sober, so answering that question in the past tense there is easy. But at this party, I imagine the group will be a little less fluent in the language of falling apart.

On the night of the party, I arrive late so I won't have to navigate the cocktail hour for very long before dinner. I don't ask Jean who she has me seated next to, because I don't want her to worry. But of course *I* worry. During cocktails I talk to Jean's daughters, who are always friendly. At dinner I sit next to an exquisite middle-aged woman, dressed in a perfect suit and deftly arranged scarf. Just as she introduces herself, a waiter comes and asks if we'd like red or white wine. She places her elegant hand and long fingers over the top of the empty wine glass next to her dinner plate and says, *I won't be drinking tonight.* After I blurt, *Same here,* she places that same hand on my shoulder and says, *I gather you've had quite a year. Welcome to the rooms.* How many times had I been convinced there was a dark conspiracy of intricately placed people observing, entrapping, stalking, and circling? So many. Now, with this kind, sober woman sitting next to me in the thicket of a challenging dinner party, I experience the flip side of this paranoia—the opposite of all that wild-minded *supernatural aid*

dread, the feeling instead that there are forces conspiring on my behalf, placing people in my way at precisely the right moments to guide me on whatever path I should be on. Like a blubbering imbecile, I grab her hand and say, *You have no idea how happy I am that you're here.* She asks what meetings I go to and she knows The Library well—a former sponsee of hers goes there regularly. *Madge?* she asks. *Have you heard of her?* It turns out she was—pedigree of pedigrees—Madge's first sponsor. It was a beautiful dinner.

Early in the summer Annie and I begin to meet every Saturday at various meetings. We try one and then another and always get together for coffee after. She graduates from The Library before I do. In September she gets a job teaching performing arts to kids in the Bronx during the week. Three years later she arranges to perform a showcase for the faculty at her graduate school and, at last, receives her MFA. Once she goes back to work, Saturdays become the only time I see her. Aside from the occasional Broadway musical and dinner at the Carnegie Deli, they still are.

It won't be until November that I begin to think about going back to work, and when I do, I am—out of the blue—offered a job at a literary agency. The very thing I puzzled

and panicked and stressed and moaned about since the day I
returned to New York all those months ago—a job, work,
my career, money—solves itself without my doing a thing. *I
told you so,* Jack gloats on the phone when I tell him. *All you
had to do was get honest, get sober, and offer help to a few addicts and alcoholics along the way. The rest took care of itself.* I
accept the job but with two requests: that I start in March instead of right away and that I'm free to leave the office every
afternoon to attend a two o'clock meeting. They agree, and
until that first day of work I spend the remaining months as
I have since April: gym, three meetings a day, dog run with
Polly, *Oprah*, and seeing as many alcoholics and addicts in recovery as I can find.

After the dinner at Mary Ann's, Asa drifts away. Still, I call
him on my anniversary every year to thank him for helping me get sober and ask him to call back and let me know
how he's doing. For the first few years he does, and we exchange messages for a while until we give up and another
year passes. This year I call and don't hear back from him.
I call a few more times, and still nothing. I give up and
weeks later I overhear someone say they heard he had gone
out, that he was drinking again. I call him right away and
leave another message, but again, not a peep. A few weeks
later I decide to call from the BlackBerry I've been given at

work and not the cell phone he's used to. Just as I hoped, he picks up. I don't recognize his voice. It's different—quicker, tighter—and by the sound of it anything but happy to hear from me. He does not ask how I am or what's going on in my life. He does not ask one question during the entire phone call. He tells me he's drinking and using coke recreationally and that he's happier, more confident, and having more sex than he was when he was sober. He reminds me that coke and booze were never his problems, heroin was, and he's able to manage it. He tells me that the meetings are a cult and require the people who go to them to agree that they're defective, and he doesn't have any use for that kind of thinking anymore. When I finally get a word in, I ask him to be careful and awkwardly remind him that buying coke is illegal and that I don't want him to get arrested. This sets him off and he yells that doctors and psychiatrists are breaking more laws than dealers and tells me not to call if I'm only going to lecture him or try to persuade him to get sober or go to a meeting. *Don't call me*, he says, and it feels like a punch. *Don't call me*, he says in the voice that is not the voice I knew—the one that coaxed me off the street, charmed drugs out of my hands, told me how the rooms and the people in them saved his life, talked me to sleep on the phone the night after my first relapse, told me not to give up, and asked me, the night we first met at the New Venus diner, to meet him at The Library the next day.

I am in the lobby of a movie theater on Third Avenue and 11th Street when Asa hangs up. Soon after, Cy arrives. *You OK?* she asks. *You look like you've seen a ghost.* It takes a few seconds before I can answer. I still can't believe what I've just heard. *I'm not sure,* I say, *but I think I just have.* I have not seen or heard from Asa since.

———

Heather shows up at The Library later that year. She raises her hand and counts one day. She relapses, returns, and relapses again. She has the same gift her sister has and when she tells her story—plainly, powerfully, honestly—everyone strains to hear. Polly's parents come to town, and we all go to breakfast at the diner on Seventh Avenue and 15th Street. Heather shows up half an hour late, high, belligerent, shouting about her boss, taxes, stingy tips, and until the bill is paid no one but she speaks. She comes back into the rooms, counts days again, and then disappears. Eventually she loses her job and, not long after, the rent-controlled apartment on St. Mark's Place. Polly allows her to move into her apartment in Astoria and sleep on the couch under one condition: no alcohol or drugs in the place. For the most part, she's complied.

There is a time, later, years later—after I've completed, with my sponsor's help, an unflinching review of my behavior before getting sober—when I begin to face the people I did harm to. Some I haven't seen in a long time—six, eighteen years—and some I may have seen the day before. One by one, I sit before them and read what I spent days writing—describing the harm I caused, offering to make the wrong right, if possible, and asking what I left out—and each time, when it's the moment for the person I am addressing to respond, what each one says is nothing I expect. Each time, I walk away feeling—at the edges—gratitude, relief, compassion, but at the center what can only be described as love. For a while the world will appear more as it is and less as I make it, and I will have a new courage to face the remaining wreckage of the past. I was an active addict and alcoholic for over twenty-three years. The list of people I harmed is long, and I have only scratched the surface.

Seven months after our Labor Day evening on the pier, Elliot and I break up. There is a night when it is clear that it is over, and I name it, and then cry for the first time since that morning in Lotto's kitchen. I cry uncontrollably, outlandishly, and Elliot, as he had when we were together, sits by my side, holds my hand until I can pull it together. We don't see each other for over a year, and then slowly, gradually, we begin to meet again as friends, as we do now, on tennis courts, with racquets in our hands, and between us, a speeding ball, a net.

Noah and I get back together. Something I give up wanting suddenly arrives, again, and with much hope. But it is clear from the very start—though it takes us both a year to accept—that in order to work, our relationship needs me to be an active addict and alcoholic, that the thing we thought tearing us apart all those years was actually what was holding us together. Without that dark glue, we come apart. I learn from him later, after we break up, that there was more to the dark glue than I knew. Of course he had his own battles, of course he struggled with his own demons that had nothing to do with me. I was too mired in my own to see, too invested in his being what I needed him to be to recognize him as he was. But all that comes out later, in fits and starts, and even then it takes a long time for me to believe.

Not so long ago, Noah and I run into each other at the Knickerbocker. Cy and I show up there, late, after seeing a movie nearby. Noah is sitting across from the bar, at a corner table, with his boyfriend. I haven't seen him for months, though we've spoken and e-mailed and in our way stayed in touch. He doesn't see us at first, and for a long time remains undistracted from his very engaged, very focused conversation. When he sees us, he quickly stands to come over. He crosses the room—this room that held so many of our best and worst nights—and slows before reaching our table, recognizing something as he does. He stops and turns to the side slightly, gesturing to the bar, to the restaurant, out to the street, and back to us. *Hi, Bill,* he says, a big smile on his face, holding out his hands as if to contain every last awful, ridiculous inch and minute of our shared history. *Hi, Noah,* I say. And we laugh, finally.

Lotto gets kicked out of the rehab in California. Somehow a stolen car is involved, but he will avoid arrest and prison and end up—after a year and a half of living at home and relapsing and finally being cut off from financial support— back in another rehab in Georgia. This one sticks. He stays there for a year and continues on in a nearby sober-living community for another year. I will get one message in all this time that fills me in on the ups and downs. A few months ago I see him on the street with a tall, tough-looking friend of his from Georgia. He has two years sober and is in town to visit his parents for a few days before going back. *My addict ass can't be here long,* he says in the same Mulberry-Street-meets-boarding-school voice. *And when it is, I bring protection,* he laughs, nodding to his muscled buddy. He tells me the women in Georgia are hot but lazy, and about a meeting down the street from the apartment he's just moved to. *It's a club. We have a flat-screen TV and a pool table, and it's seltzer and fucking Pepsi but it's cool.* Before we say good-bye, he gives me his cell phone number—the same one he's had for the last two years. *Some kind of record,* I say, and we both laugh. As of this writing, his phone number has not changed.

___

Annie gets married. The wedding is less than a week after Noah and I break up, over a year after I've been back at work, and the ceremony and the reception take place on a sloping field next to a lake in Ithaca, New York. I drive to the wedding with Rafe, the wildly articulate guy from The Library who never quite becomes a close friend in the way Annie and Luke have, but whose knowing looks and *Hi, Bill*s have become a steady, counted-on part of my recovery. He agrees to be my sponsor when Jack moves upstate to teach at a small college. Rafe and I stop for lunch on the way, during which my sister Kim calls, upset because my younger brother has been the cause of another drunken brawl and, after, an ugly scene at my mother's house. I feel helpless. I know what to say and how to act with other ad-

dicts and alcoholics, like Polly, but I have no clue what to
do for my brother or how to help my family. I tell Rafe
about my family, my struggling brother, breaking up with
Noah, being single, without romantic possibilities or en-
tanglements for the first time since high school—and he
listens. I tell him I feel lonelier and more alone than I can
ever remember feeling. He reminds me that feelings aren't
facts (another one of Jack's old expressions that I used to
cringe at but now cling to), and that I'm sober, which means
I may be low but I'm not lost, powerless but not useless.
*Stop feeling sorry for yourself,* he snaps, and not for the first
time suggests the simple, surefire solution for self-pity that
on my own I always forget: *Call another addict with less time
sober than you.* And so I do.

I check into a hotel that is also one of the tallest buildings
in Ithaca. I am assigned, because of some accident in the
booking, a large suite on the top floor, and it seems like the
emptiest room I have ever seen. My friend John, who moved
to Asia a few years before and whom I'd mostly lost touch
with, calls from Saipan the next morning and we stay on the
phone for hours before I leave for the wedding. I tell him everything that's happened over the last two years—returning
to New York after rehab, relapsing, The Library, reaching
ninety days, Elliot, starting a job at a literary agency, getting

back together with Noah and ending it, finally, just days ago. I tell him, as I look out the window to the hills that surround Ithaca and rise shoulder to shoulder against an enormous blue sky, that I'm thirty-six, a year and ten months sober, and on my own. At the reception later, surrounded by Rafe and Polly and Annie, at a table crowded with seltzers and Diet Cokes and coffee cups, I know that I've never been less alone in my life.

Asa arrives late, as the procession music begins, and leaves early. We wave to each other as he's being seated, but after Annie kisses her new husband and the rice is thrown, he disappears. I look for him at the reception after, but he is gone before I have a chance to say good-bye.

Polly and I walk down to the lake and sit on a dock as the sun goes down. She is wearing a green dress and her loose hair shines in the late day light. She looks healthier and more beautiful than I've ever seen her. She has a year and four months sober that night. She has just over five years now. *Here we are, Crackhead,* she says, the way she always does. We look out over the lake. Wind skims the surface, swallows dart and swoop above the shimmering water, and the first stars stitch the sky. The dock sways beneath us, laughter sparks above the thumping music of the reception, and neither of us makes a sound as the sun finds its way home, again, behind the formidable hills of Ithaca. I know exactly what she means. Here we are.

# Close

*I had the best gin and tonic in the world in the lobby of the Mandarin Oriental Hotel.* My friend John says these words as we're sitting on the terrace of a house we've rented on a small island in Thailand. It's early January and we've come here for a month to work—him on a book project and a magazine article, me on a book I've been writing for two and half years, the one you are reading now. We've spent four weeks working from morning to night interrupted only by meals cooked by two shy women who arrive in the morning and leave in the evening and blush when we praise and thank them for the delicious food. It's dinnertime now. Fading sun and stars commingle in the early evening sky as the women load plates with curried vegetables and steamed rice.

I've told John I've booked a room at the Mandarin Oriental in Bangkok on the way back to New York and he tosses a memory of a gin and tonic he drank in his early twenties into the air as casually as he would a receipt in the trash. But I catch it and hold on. This drink he consumed decades ago now sits on the dinner table between us, and nothing else holds my attention—not the last panels of light sliding along the rippling sea below, the flickering candles, the magnificent food. Nothing exists but the drink—its sleek vessel of glass, its magic contents, and the legendary hotel it was consumed in. Over the next four days I imagine the perspiration on the rim of the glass, the thrum of hotel lobby glamour, the garnish of the greenest lime. On the morning I leave for Bangkok I finish a draft of the book, type the last lines, the ones you just read. I send the document to my editor by e-mail and a few hours later ride a longboat to Phuket, where I catch a plane to Bangkok. John will arrive a day after I do and we have planned to meet in an overpriced restaurant along the river to celebrate our last night in Thailand.

When I arrive in Bangkok I hail a cab in front of the arrivals terminal. The driver is young—twenty-five, maybe thirty—and after I tell him which hotel to take me to, he asks the following questions: *You like boys? You like girls? You like drugs?* My answer, without thinking, without thought of any kind, as reflexive as a leg shooting straight after a doctor's tap on the knee, is this: *Yes.* When we pull up to the hotel the driver scribbles a number on a piece of paper and hands it to me. *Tonight,* he says. *You call tonight.* I nod and take the paper and put it in my pocket. What am I thinking as I get out of the taxi with this number, the first of its kind I've held in almost six years? Nothing. I am thinking nothing.

The lobby of the Mandarin Oriental. It is thrumming, as I had imagined, but it is modern and familiar and Americans are everywhere. I am taken to my room, where a middle-aged man in a hotel uniform shows me the bathroom, the various electrical outlets, the bar, which I see has only Smirnoff vodka, and the balcony overlooking the river. He takes my credit card and looks at my passport. I sign something and he leaves. It is now late afternoon and the sun is like a chunk of molten lava hanging in the sky and the air around it is hazy and orange. From the balcony I see boats crowding the river and dozens of hotel guests pacing the terraces below. Bangkok seems caught in something heavier than air, everything and everyone pushing sluggishly through the thick atmosphere. Planes labor across the sky so slowly they seem about to drop from exhaustion.

The ice bucket above the bar is full. The butler buzzes my room to find out if I need anything. I ask him if they have Stolichnaya and he says he'll go see. On the bed my phone buzzes to signal it has received an e-mail. I don't go to it. It buzzes again and I lean against the desk and wait for the butler to return. Ice is bursting from the bucket. I've never seen ice so abundant, so refreshing. I fill a glass. A thick, low glass, the kind my father drank scotch from when I was a kid. There are no limes in the place but there is a fruit basket and in it an orange that I slice a small wedge from. I squeeze a bit of juice onto the ice and shove the rind between the ice and the glass. No butler. No Stoli. My phone buzzes again and I grab the bottle of Smirnoff and pour the drink. There it is. Vodka not gin. Orange not lime. Smirnoff not Ketel One. Smirnoff not Stoli. By no means the best vodka in the world. By no means even the second best. But it's here. And no one else is. No one is watching. No one is waiting for me and it's been almost six years. A drink, just one, on the balcony of the Mandarin Oriental Hotel. Why does this feel necessary? Why has it seemed inevitable since John uttered those words four days ago? I do not know. But it does. And so I pick up the drink, put the glass to my lips, and swallow a mouthful of vodka. It tastes like poison. Cold, foul, thick. Is it because it's Smirnoff? Is it because there is an orange and not a lime? A balcony and not a lobby? Or is it because I haven't had a drink in so many years? Agitated, I drink more. I pour a second and a third, and the vodka tastes no better. I don't feel anything more than a gathering heaviness. A slowness like the air around me. A dulling. In the room I pour a fourth and return to the balcony. Six floors up. I palm the piece of paper. It's too soon to call. It is not night. How many drinks until it will be late enough to call? I can see the fuzzy mural of the near future: the cab ride, the cash machine, the bag of crack or its equivalent, the stems, the lighter, the skin, calling for more, bottles of vodka, the dizzying crash. I don't want it but I want it. But want feels more like acceptance of a kind of sentence. There is no turning back. I've begun something that will be finished, and as I look down the six stories to the terrace and alley below, I know that death is where this will go. Hours ago I sent off a manuscript about early recovery, how difficult getting and staying sober is, how it cannot be done alone. Alone, I down most of the fourth drink. I don't bother with the orange now. Dying in Bangkok. It feels suddenly like the most logical, inevitable outcome. The cabdriver, the phone number, this terrace, this drink, the coming night and all it will entail—each piece clicks into place, the intended path becomes visible. It's clear now. The book is finished, my use expired. A new slow wind moves warm air across the balcony and lights blink across the river from hotels and apartment buildings. My death will remind people how serious addiction is, how lethal. Death will be useful.

I finger the scrap of paper. I finish the drink, which tastes just as awful as the first. My phone buzzes again. Before I pour a fifth drink, before I call that number, I go to the bed and check the phone to see who has been sending me messages. *Hey, you around? Free to talk? What's up? Can we talk?* Four messages—each one from my new sponsee. The one who relapsed while I was in Thailand, the one who has seen me at The Library every day for months and because of that asked me to be his sponsor. The one who, more than anyone else I've met, reminds me of myself in early sobriety. The determination to appear in control, the relentless relapsing, the recurring courtship with death. There he is, reaching out from the other side of the world. And here I am, about to pour a fifth vodka. About to call the number in my pocket.

I look again at his messages. So persistent, so willing. Finally, after months of relapsing and dodging his former sponsor, he is asking for help. Asking *me* for help. Reaching out to end the agony he's thrashed around in for years. Agony I know, agony I had been released from. I close the phone and put it back on the bed. And just like that, it's over. I'm done. Whatever started days ago on the terrace with John and led to four vodkas in this hotel room has stopped. I rip up the piece of paper, grab my hotel room key, and head for the door. I walk through the lobby and out to the front

drive and into the street. I call my brother. It is morning in
Maine where he lives and I leave him a message. I tell him
an almost-truth. I tell him I almost picked up, almost drank,
almost used. I walk until I find a guy selling large bottles of
water. I buy one and dump half of it on my head and down
the rest in a few long gulps. I walk through the hurdy-gurdy
streets of Bangkok, past the bars with boys and girls for sale,
past fruit stands and T-shirt vendors, past the empty streets
in the now shut business districts. I walk until I am about to
collapse and signal a tuk-tuk, a cross between a moped and
a rickshaw, and tell the driver the name of the hotel. When I
enter the room for the second time that day I am as far from
wanting a drink or a drug as I can be.

The next night, with green and red and white fireworks
streaking above the river, I tell John every part of the story
except for the drinking. I expand the almost-truth I left on
my brother's voice mail. I tell him I read my sponsee's messages and didn't drink, and as I do I feel that old distance
return, that old barrier rise up between me and the people
who think they know me. He suspects nothing, is an arm's
length from where I sit, but word by word he recedes further
and further away.

After I return to New York, I tell the same story to everyone at The Library and I tell the same story there twice again. The story of how I almost picked up. The story of how close I came. How close. It's the story I tell my brother, my sponsee, my family, Rafe, and everyone else close to me. I tell this story and in the space it creates between me and everyone else, a second self, a hidden one, returns. And with it the fear of being found out. The little thread of almost true gathers and braids with other threads and soon the thread is a rope and from the rope a noose that chafes and tugs, just like it always had. But no good can come from telling this, I remind myself. No good at all. I can't worry the people in my life—my family, my clients, my friends, my colleagues. I can't put the threat of relapse back on the table again, it's not fair. But I know it's not them I'm thinking of, it's me. I'm afraid of losing what I have—respect, trust, success, financial security, love; afraid of not getting what I want— more of all these things. Again, as it once did, fear shoots through every thought, every action, every minute. I sit in The Library and hear people—newly sober, long sober— talk about how once they lived in fear and now do not. They say things like *The truth will set you free,* and I think they are speaking directly to me. My sponsee, the same one whose messages stopped me in Bangkok, refuses to count days in meetings. I beg him to come to The Library and raise his hand and he refuses. *I'll go to meetings,* he says, *but I won't count days. I don't want people to know I relapsed. It's no one's business.* I tell him, again and again, he needs to come clean in the rooms, to be seen and heard there, to let people help him. I say these words and it's as if they are coming from someone else's mouth and throat and are meant for me.

A friend, not someone who struggles with drugs and alcohol, is embroiled in a complicated situation, a house of cards of deception and secrecy involving many people that is toppling in on him, and one night he comes to my apartment in desperation. There seems to be no solution, and for a while I get caught up in the faulty logic that delivered him to this mess. At first the situation appears just as hopeless as he describes. And then it's clear. The truth is the only answer, the only chance of moving ahead toward any sane future. When I say this he responds as if it is the last and least likely solution. Citing all the imagined consequences—what will be lost, what won't be gained—he rejects the idea, and I do everything I can to convince him it's the only way. *The truth will set you free,* I say cornily, passionately, and again a voice that is mine and not mine is speaking to me.

In February I go to Miami for a long weekend. It is just after the breakup of an almost-year-long relationship and getting

out of New York seems like a good idea. It is the weekend
of the Academy Awards and I invite the friends I am with
to my room to watch the show. After they leave I begin to
clean up, collect the dirty dishes, the empty glasses. I notice
a glass of white wine. It is full and untouched and perspiration beads on its rim. I pick it up and take a sip. Just like
that. The sip of wine is in my mouth and down my throat
and I recoil as if bitten by a snake. I spit the remaining wine
out of my mouth and sit down on the couch as if the sip had
happened to me, as if I am somehow its victim. I don't want
more but I know I am in trouble. I leave the room, take the
stairs down to the lobby, head out past the pool, the boardwalk, and onto the beach. Halfway between the boardwalk
and the ocean, I drop to my knees and lie down face-first in
the sand. Six years ago, at the rehab in White Plains, just a
few nights before returning to Manhattan, I lay down in a
muddy field under a raining sky and asked for help. I was
lost then. I am lost now. I don't have a plan or any answers.
I am powerless and fearful and into the damp sand I ask for
help. *Help me. Help me, God.* The answer almost six years
before was the faintest streak of light in a sky crowded with
rain clouds. The answer now is the roar of the ocean, thumping music from the hotel lounges, and the sound of teenagers
shouting in Spanish from the boardwalk.

There is a phrase I've heard at The Library and in other rooms hundreds of times. It's a phrase that sounded loudly in my ears in the months after Bangkok, after Miami: *We are only as sick as our secrets.* I missed not being sick. Eventually, weeks later, I call Annie. We hadn't spoken in months. An occasional text, a voice mail here and there. She picks up on the first ring and I tell her everything. *OK,* she says after a short silence. *OK.* We talk for a long time and as we do I feel the noose loosen, the rope go slack. As the call ends she says, *Stay close, lambchop.* And I do. I tell Luke and then John and Kim and Cy. I tell my brother and my parents and I tell Polly, who will respond without words but with the tightest hug. I tell my sponsee, who, two days later, turns up at The Library, raises his hand, and announces his day count. Three days later he does it again, and at the end of the meeting he is surrounded. I tell Rafe, who says, among other things, exactly what Annie had said and what Jack, years ago, used to say: *Stay close.*

Later, three months from that sip of wine in Miami, I will raise my hand in a meeting I rarely go to in Midtown and say, shakily but with great relief, *I have ninety days.* Three days later, at The Library, with Polly in the seat next to me, her hand on my back, I raise my hand and tell everyone in the room what happened. And now I'm telling you.

Five and a half years and then one day. For me, there are no finish lines. No recovered, just recovering. My sobriety, that delicate state that can, for years at a time, feel unshakable, is completely dependent on my connection to other alcoholics and addicts, my seeking their help and my offering it. I went to an island for a month where there were no rooms where alcoholics and addicts gather to stay sober. If we learn at the speed of pain, the painful lesson here was that I need those rooms, those addicts and alcoholics. I need them like oxygen. No matter how good, how sober, how in control I feel. There are many programs of recovery. Paid, free, anonymous, not anonymous. I don't name here which one I go to because I don't want that program held responsible for anything I do or say or write. I don't want anything to get in the way of your finding it if it can help you. Alcoholics and addicts create enough obstacles to getting sober and I don't want to add more.

If you are struggling with drugs and alcohol, go to the rooms where alcoholics and addicts go to get and stay sober. These rooms and the people in them are your best chance. Listen to them, be honest with them. Help them—even if you think you have nothing to offer. Be helped by them. Depend on them and be depended on. And if the only thing you can do is show up, do it. Then do it again. And when it's the last thing you want to do and the last place you want to go, *go*. Just go. You have no idea who you might be helping just by sitting there or who might help you. I've heard many alcoholics and addicts describe a voice that tells them to drift, to detach, to follow their own counsel and cut off. It's the same voice that told me I could be on an island for a month without meetings; suggested that a drink was better than all others — *the best* — because it happened to be in a hotel; that no good could come from telling the truth and that death was useful. In my experience only one thing has been able to quiet that voice: other alcoholics and addicts in recovery. Their voices have been louder than the one that lies, louder than my own. They have, one day at a time, guided me toward honesty, usefulness, and they have saved my life. Together, they stay sober. Together, they end years of agony and isolation. If you are struggling with drugs and alcohol, they can help you, too. Find them now.

—

# Acknowledgments

Thanks to Pat Strachan, the wisest eye, for ongoing editorial guidance; Michael Pietsch and David Young for continued support; the Dream Team at Little, Brown—Michelle Aielli, Amanda Brown, and Heather Fain—for unflagging excellence; Raffaella DeAngelis, Tracy Fisher, and the foreign-rights team at WME for being the best; Robin Robertson and Luiz Schwarcz for their rigor and care and for their friendship; Julia Eisenman, Jill Bialosky, Chris Pomeroy, Jay Knowlton, Joey Arbagey, Adam McLaughlin, Jonathan Galassi, and Kelle Groom for their time and their meticulous notes; Cy O'Neal for thieving, for movies, for more; Shaun Dolan for never blinking no matter what; John Bowe for being in the next room; Jean Stein for every magnificent voice mail and for having faith; my family—Mom, Dad, Kim, Brian, Matt, Ben, Lisa, Mark, Lillian, and Sean—for encouragement, love, and for defying gravity; Van Scott for all the days, and Jennifer Rudolph Walsh—great force, friend, agent, boss —for everything.

Thanks most of all to all the drunks and addicts who helped me get and stay sober and all those who still do.

# About the Author

Bill Clegg is a literary agent in New York. He is also the author of *Portrait of an Addict as a Young Man*.

bill-clegg.com

BACK BAY · READERS' PICK

Reading Group Guide

# NINETY DAYS

*A Memoir of Recovery*

*by*

BILL CLEGG

# A conversation with Bill Clegg

**The author of *Ninety Days* talks with Yale Breslin of *GQ*.**

*You've said that the day after you finished writing* Ninety Days, *you relapsed. Did you feel it coming? What factors do you attribute to your relapse?*

I did not see it coming; in fact I'd never felt more serene, and sober. I was on an island in southern Thailand for a month finishing *Ninety Days* (a book about recovery, of all things), and felt deeply relaxed and connected to my sobriety. But the feeling was not accurate. I was in fact the most far away (from sobriety) I'd been in the five and a half years of being sober. I was away from the AA meeting I'd go to every day, away from my sober community, not in touch with other alcoholics and addicts in recovery in the way that I am usually: by phone, over coffee, after and before meetings. I'd talked to my sponsor, and taken on a new sponsee while I was away, but basically I'd disconnected from my sober family for the first time in sobriety. There is an expression that people in recovery hear and say all the time: "Feelings aren't facts," and in this case it was all too true.

*Do you feel that you're finished (for now) telling your story about addiction and recovery? Or do you see another book that documents another phase of the puzzle?*

I think these two books say more than I ever expected to say on addiction and recovery. If there is anything more I'll tell my cat, Benny.

*Your musical tastes changed and progressed throughout the years, and you've mentioned that Rachael Yamagata's music had a profound influence on your recovery. How so?*

I listened to Rachael's first album, *Happenstance*, during the year I spent unemployed, going to three meetings a day, getting sober. They were sad songs about loss and grief and moving on, and they sounded like I felt…especially in the first few months of returning to New York after rehab.

*What was your first introduction to her as an artist?*

I was in a coffee shop on Jane Street and heard the first few notes on a piano to a song of hers called "Quiet," and they were the saddest, most mournful notes I'd ever heard.

I thought: There I am; that's me. And I went home and downloaded *Happenstance* and listened to that album until I couldn't anymore.

*In some ways, is it hard now to listen to her music?*

I didn't listen to *Happenstance* for a long time after I got sober and went back to work. When I was writing *Ninety Days,* I began to listen to those songs again as a way of remembering. So I went back in for a while, and wallowed.

*You have formed a relationship with her—when did this start? How did you meet?*

I met Rachael recently to do a reading and interview at Barnes and Noble. The format was that I would read a little, she'd play some songs, and we'd be interviewed in between. The first song she played was "Reason Why," which was one of the songs I listened to over and over. It begins with the lyrics, "I think about how it might have been...," which, in the early period of sobriety, was a haunting speculation I'd torture myself with. If I hadn't relapsed, if I'd stayed sober and not spiraled into the two-month bender that ruined everything. What if, What if... There is another lyric later in the song, "So I will head out alone and hope for the best, we can pat ourselves on the back and say that we tried..." I imagined many times that I'd have to leave New York, that

I'd return to the small town in Connecticut I'd started out in, or go to live with my sister in Maine, and that I'd have to give up on New York, that I'd blown my chance here.

*Have you always been into music?*

I was obsessed with Bob Dylan throughout high school and college. I still am.

*If you look back on your life—addiction, recovery, relapse, documentation, sobriety—how have you seen your musical tastes change?*

I was pretty strict in high school about who I would listen to. Musicians like Neil Young, Cat Stevens, Bob Dylan, Joni Mitchell...who were, in my opinion, great writers. The music mattered, but it held hands with the lyrics, and the personality was, overall, unsullied. In the little rural town I grew up in, I missed out on the pop music of the time, the eighties, and now enjoy it in retrospect. It's as an adult that I've opened up to dance, hip-hop, R&B, and even big pop songs. But I guess I'm still drawn to singer-songwriters who have the voice, and conjure the lyrics and music into songs that seem like soul cries. Lately I listen a lot to Justin Vernon, Antony, Martha Wainwright, Brandi Carlile, and Feist.

*Now that sobriety is one of your marked characteristics, do you feel that that helps or deters you from keeping sober?*

It helps, though it wasn't the reason or goal in writing the books. I spent the first thirty-three years of my life with secrets, and lots of them. I spent a great deal of energy worrying over what people thought and obscuring the things I was ashamed of...trying to appear what I thought was normal. My relationship to drugs and alcohol, and the depths my dependency on them brought me to, were the last things I ever wanted to be exposed. By writing about these things I not only lightened a long-carried load but, I hope, became of use to people who have, and who still do, struggle in the way that I struggled. In my first year of getting sober, I learned that being of use to other alcoholics and addicts (seeing how my experience could be helpful) was not only the surprising benefit of everything that led to my getting sober, but also the way I stayed sober. Writing these books was not something I initially thought would be part of my ongoing sobriety, but over time, as I get letters and e-mails about how something in one of them was helpful to someone, it reminds me of the usefulness I feel when working with others in recovery. Anything that reconnects me to the feeling that by staying clean I can be helpful to another alcoholic or drug addict helps keep me sober.

This interview appears courtesy of Yale Breslin.

# Questions and topics for discussion

1. Bill Clegg's friend Lotto was in rehab for drug use ten times before he was twenty-two. Finally, a successful recovery in Georgia led him to move there from a privileged life in Manhattan. What does his story tell you about the tenacity of addiction? Does it give you more empathy toward addicts?

2. One reviewer praised *Ninety Days* for being singular as a recovery book that is also about relapse. Did you think in the end that any of the people introduced in the book were fully recovered? Were you surprised by Asa's relapse?

3. Have you had experiences in your own life that didn't involve substance abuse but compared in some ways to addiction?

4. "It's the jaggedness of getting off the drugs—finding the language for that—that gives *Ninety Days* its stark

power," wrote Michael Klein in *Lambda Literary*. How did Bill Clegg's prose style contribute to your response to his memoir?

5. Do you think *Ninety Days* can serve as a cautionary tale? Or that it can help readers who are dealing with past or current drug or alcohol addiction? If so, how?

6. What fundamental shift in the way he related to other people and himself did Bill Clegg make to attain sobriety? How did Polly and others in "the rooms" save his life—and he theirs, for whatever length of time?

7. The author still attends meetings at least once a day to maintain his years of sobriety. How can a person with an important career and many friends find time for such a commitment? Do you think the time consumed by addiction is any less demanding?

8. In an interview, Bill Clegg has said, "That first burst of sobriety, which people in recovery often describe as a pink cloud—I have never felt more exhilarated in my life." Could breaking any habit or addiction of your own lead you to such happiness?

## Also by Bill Clegg

# PORTRAIT OF AN ADDICT AS A YOUNG MAN

### *A Memoir*

"Clegg may not have been able to control his demons, but he is utterly in charge of this material, with a voice that is knowing and self-deprecating in exactly the right measure."

—Jonathan Van Meter, *Vogue*

"Rings true in brutal, blunt strokes."

—David Carr, *New York Times Book Review*

"Bill Clegg has written an exceptionally fine addition to a genre largely bereft of style, intelligence, and moral complexity....It's plain to see that people stuck by him because they enjoy his company, because he inspires fierce loyalty. Now, at last, Bill Clegg seems capable of believing it."

—Kirk Davis Swinehart, *Chicago Tribune*

"It turns out there is room on the shelf for one more addiction memoir....Clegg spares no one's feelings, least of all his own; it's not the brutality that makes this worthwhile but rather the strange beauty of the stream-of-consciousness prose. We're voyeurs, as helpless to stop the carnage as the author himself."
—Mickey Rapkin, *GQ*

**Back Bay Books • Available wherever paperbacks are sold**